The Macat Library

世界思想宝库钥匙丛书

解析克利福德·格尔茨

《文化的解释》

AN ANALYSIS OF

CLIFFORD GEERTZ'S

THE INTERPRETATION OF CULTURES

Abena Dadze-Arthur ◎ 著

陈运香 ◎ 译

上海外语教育出版社
外教社 SHANGHAI FOREIGN LANGUAGE EDUCATION PRESS

MACAT

目 录

CONTENTS

引 言

要 点

- 美国文化人类学家 * 克利福德·格尔茨，在太平洋岛国印度尼西亚 * 进行了大量的实地研究，于 1973 年出版了其论文集《文化的解释》。2006 年，格尔茨辞世。

- 文化人类学研究人类文化的差异。很多人认为格尔茨是美国最重要的文化人类学家。

- 格尔茨认为，文化 * 是一种共有意义体系，应该通过解释文化象征（比如艺术和神话）对其进行研究。《文化的解释》一书正是对此领域进行界定。尽管公众常常对这本书存在误解，然而这本书仍然是跨学科研究者引用最多的著作之一。

克利福德·格尔茨其人

克利福德·格尔茨，文化人类学家，最为人知的著作是 1973 年出版的《文化的解释》一书。1926 年 8 月 23 日，格尔茨出生于美国旧金山。格尔茨年仅 3 岁时，父母离婚。之后，他随养父母在加利福尼亚的乡下生活。17 岁时，格尔茨加入了美国海军。在服役两年后，格尔茨于 1945 年二战 * 结束之际离开了海军。

二战之后，格尔茨就读于俄亥俄州的安提阿学院，获得了退伍军人权利法案的资助（美国政府对二战退伍军人提供的专项资助），1950 年毕业，获得哲学学位。后来，他进入知名的哈佛大学研究生院学习，师从两位知名学者：一位是人类学教授克莱德·克拉克洪 *，一位是社会学 * 教授塔尔科特·帕森斯 *。1956 年，格尔茨获得人类学博士学位。

在之后的 15 年里，格尔茨先后撰写了数篇论文，最终收集在

《文化的解释》一书中。这些论文展示了他在印度尼西亚的巴厘岛、爪哇岛、苏门答腊岛三个岛屿的实地研究中形成的观点。这段时期，格尔茨与自己的第一任妻子希尔德雷德·斯托里·格尔茨*一起进行研究，她同样也是一位知名的人类学家。

1970年，格尔茨成为新泽西州普林斯顿高等研究学院社会科学教授，在此工作了30年之久，度过了自己的余生。克利福德和希尔德雷德婚后没有孩子，在共同生活了32年后离异。后来，格尔茨与凯伦·布鲁*结婚，凯伦·布鲁也是一位人类学家，两人育有两个孩子。

格尔茨于2006年10月30日在一次心脏手术中去世。曾与格尔茨共事过的文化人类学家理查德·艾伦·施韦德*评价道，"格尔茨为人谦逊，甚至有点内向，踌躇不决，但与人交往时却又风趣健谈。"[1]

《文化的解释》的主要内容

《文化的解释》于1973年出版，是一部"文化理论专著"。[2]这本书正式并系统地解释了什么是文化，以及我们应该如何研究文化。这本书促使了人们对人类学学科进行重新界定，同时推动了文化人类学的形成。文化人类学研究不同民族和社会之间的文化差异，以及人们的行为方式、传播方式和交往方式。

格尔茨将文化定义为"一种用象征形式表达传承概念的体系"。[3]换言之，他认为文化是含有特殊意义的象征和符号的有序集合。例如，垂死的耶稣被钉在十字架上的雕像，是一种带有宗教意义的象征，是宗教文化体系的一部分。即使是不信教的，不属于这个特定文化体系中的人，也能认出这个象征。

格尔茨基于自己的文化概念，认为我们应该使用特殊的方式来研究文化。在《文化的解释》中，针对如何开展研究，他提出了两个核心观点：

第一，他主张，人类学家惟有通过观察人们是如何使用象征、符号、象征性行为、仪式等来进行表达的，才能真正地理解文化。例如，对基督徒而言，在做礼拜时吃面包和喝葡萄酒是一种象征性行为，象征着吃耶稣的肉、喝耶稣的血。因此，具有这种相同文化的人们，会使用这些象征性行为来庆祝上帝用爱让耶稣由死亡转向新生。

第二，格尔茨认为，人类学家应该从相关民族的视角进行文化研究。他相信，"文化和民族有其自身特征，人类学家应该学会与其交流，并对其进行解释。"4 换言之，文化应该从文化内部的视角来解释。

这意味着，人类学家应该像生活在该文化中的人一样解读象征或象征性行为的意义，惟有这样，才能将意义进行翻译并传递给外界。格尔茨将此过程称为解释性方法 *。不同的群体在其社交世界中构建了不同的现实，解释性研究者应该对这些现实进行解释和阐述。

当然，所有的解释必须根植于某一特定的时刻。这些解释要与某一具体的时间、语境和形势相一致。当然，对话可能造成解释在一定程度上被修改或重新定义。正因如此，格尔茨提出的解释性方法表明：要想了解一个民族，研究者必须通过这个民族的视野来观察世界，只有这样，他们才能作出可靠的解释。

《文化的解释》的学术价值

《文化的解释》的出版，使格尔茨成为 20 世纪 60 年代"象征人类学"或解释人类学运动的"首席代言人"。5 对很多人而言，无论在人类学学科领域内还是领域之外，《文化的解释》不仅展现了格尔茨的研究，也解释了文化人类学的总体研究。[6]

《文化的解释》也影响了当代文化人类学的发展。格尔茨论述道，促进研究者和研究主体之间的对话至关重要。这就要求研究者对象征和象征性行为的意义进行仔细观察，并对使用者进行访谈。通过这种方式，人类学家可以更全面、更精确地了解他们的考察对象。同时，它还能帮助人类学家更好地了解人们是如何理解自身、理解他人以及理解他们周围的世界的。更进一步，这种理解又有利于人类学家对社会作出更加全面、更富有代表性的解释。

《文化的解释》为我们展示了一种理解不同文化的方法。[7]鉴于世界上文化、道德、科技、政治等方面的多样性日益增加，理解我们之间的差异在今天仍像 20 世纪 60 年代格尔茨工作时一样重要和适时。正如颇具影响力的文化人类学家雪莉·奥特纳*所言，格尔茨的这本书"价值永存"，人人适用。[8]

《文化的解释》为 2007 年《文化心理学手册》中被引用最多的著作。[9]《纽约时报文学副刊》称之为"二战以来最重要的 100 部著作之一"。[10]对于想要解释世界上人们行为的意义的人来说，这本书依旧是不二之选。[11]

---

1. 理查德·施韦德：《克利福德·詹姆斯·格尔茨：传记回忆录（1926—2006）》，哥伦比亚特区华盛顿：国家科学院出版社，第 5 页，登录日期 2015 年 11 月 2 日，https://www.sss.ias.edu/files/pdfs/Geertz_NAS-6-10-10.pdf。

2. 克利福德·格尔茨:《文化的解释》，第 2 版，纽约：基础书局，2000 年，第 viii 页。

3. 格尔茨:《文化的解释》，第 89 页。

4. 安德鲁·亚罗："克利福德·格尔茨，文化人类学家，80 岁辞世"，《纽约时报》，2006 年 11 月 1 日，登录日期 2015 年 12 月 8 日，http://www.nytimes.com/2006/11/01/obituaries/01geertz.html?pagewanted=print&_r=0。

5. 理查德·施韦德："克利福德·格尔茨的果断与不决"，《通识》第 13 卷，2007 年春秋刊第 2—3 期，第 191—205 页。

6. 理查德·施韦德和拜伦·古德:《同事眼中的克利福德·格尔茨》，芝加哥：芝加哥大学出版社，2005 年。

7. 施韦德："克利福德·格尔茨的果断与不决"，第 203 页。

8. 雪莉·奥特纳："专题：'文化'的命运：格尔茨及其他"，《再现》第 59 卷，1997 年，第 7 页。

9. 施韦德："克利福德·格尔茨的果断与不决"，第 203 页。

10. 亚罗："克利福德·格尔茨"。

11. 参见奥特纳："专题"，第 7 页。

第一部分：学术渊源

1 作者生平与历史背景

要点 ✥══

- 学者们认为，《文化的解释》是解释人类学 * 的奠基性文本之一。解释人类学是一种人类学研究方法，主张各民族和文化应该具有自身特色，人类学家应该学会如何向外界解释文化意义。

- 格尔茨的研究受多个学科影响，这一点从他毕生对跨学科 * 试验的热情可以看出来；"跨学科"是指运用不同学科的目标和方法进行的整合性研究。

- 到了 20 世纪 60 年代，人类学试图远离其殖民主义 *（19 世纪欧洲在政治和经济上的对外领土扩张）起源，并重新确定自身研究领域，即探索人们看待自己和世界的方式。

为何要读这部著作？

克利福德·格尔茨的《文化的解释》（1973）一书主张应该对人类学研究采取解释性方法，至今仍是人类学学科的学生必读的文献。

在这本书中，格尔茨提出解释人类学有两个目的：第一，要通过生长在特定文化中的人的视角来观察世界；第二，将由此获得的洞见传递给该文化之外的人们——这就是著名的解释主义。

研究文化的解释性方法彻底改变了人类学的领域。格尔茨是提出"某个文化之外的人应该通过理解生活在该文化中的人的主观看法对该文化（即来自其他文化的人所理解的世界）进行研究"的第一代学者之一。在此之前，人们普遍相信，人类学家应该作为独立的观察者，"从非本民族文化者的角度客观地"研究该文化。[1] 备受尊敬的社会人类学家 *（研究社会结构及其在人类文化中的作用的学者）阿兰姆·延戈扬 * 对东南亚颇有研究，他认为，《文化的解释》提出了一种新的人类学形式。格尔茨的研究方法与他同时代学者所倡导的人类学研究方法差异很大。[2]

《文化的解释》产生的影响超出了人类学的范畴，波及社会科学和人文学科。1973 年《文化的解释》刚一出版，学术界便认识到其重要性。仅过了一年，这本书就获得了 1974 年美国社会学协会颁发的索罗金奖。2000 年，当《文化的解释》一书再版时，《纽约时报》称之为"二战以来最重要的 100 部著作之一"。[3] 然而，普通大众却从未充分认识到格尔茨这本书的重要性。

> "我要特别感谢三所杰出的学术机构，它们为我提供的那种学术研究环境，我深信世界上现在没有任何地方能比得上：哈佛大学社会关系学院，我曾在那里求学；芝加哥大学人类学系，我曾在那里任教十年；普林斯顿大学高等研究学院，我现在工作的地方。"
>
> —— 克利福德·格尔茨：《文化的解释》

作者生平

1926 年，克利福德·格尔茨出生于美国加利福尼亚州旧金山市。3 岁时，父母离异。随后，被送往加利福尼亚乡下由养父母抚养。17 岁时，他加入了美国海军，从 1943 年至 1945 年在二战中服役。

服役期满之后，格尔茨在俄亥俄州的安提阿学院学习哲学，得到了哲学家乔治·盖格 * 的指导。1950 年毕业后，格尔茨申请攻读哈佛大学新成立的社会关系学院的博士学位。[4] 这个跨学科学院有两位知名的美国学者：一位是社会学家塔尔科特·帕森斯，另一位是文化人类学家克莱德·克拉克洪。社会学研究人类社会的本质和历史，而文化人类学则是对构成"文化"的人类信仰和实践进行研究。格尔茨后来提到，哈佛大学这所新学院独特的学术文化感染了他，使他对"跨学科试验产生了极大兴趣"。[5] 从此，这种兴趣伴他终生，成为他工作中不可或缺的一部分。

1960年，格尔茨受聘于知名的芝加哥大学人类学系。在芝加哥大学任教的十年里，格尔茨倡导自己独特的文化概念。[6]1970年，格尔茨任职于普林斯顿大学，成为高等研究学院的社会科学教授，2000年被聘为荣誉教授，在那里度过了他的余生。在普林斯顿大学，格尔茨确立了自己的地位，高等研究学院院长彼得·戈达德称其为"20世纪重要的知识分子之一"。[7]他最有影响力的著作包括：《爪哇的宗教》（1960）、《巴厘的人、时间与行为》（1966）、《文化的解释》（1973）、《地方性知识：解释人类学论文集》（1983）和《论著与生活：作为作者的人类学家》（1988）。[8]

创作背景

克利福德·格尔茨在20世纪60年代撰写了《文化的解释》一书，这一时期社会、政治动荡不安，其主要特征是后殖民主义*（一种关于殖民时期遗留下来的各种社会、哲学和语言等问题的理论思潮）和社会革命*（活跃的、普遍的对现行社会制度表达不满的方式）。这些革命之后，"人类学已经被殖民时代的问题弄得支离破碎。"[9]

要了解这段历史，我们需要回顾17世纪和18世纪。殖民时代的人类学家致力于对殖民地的文化进行"科学"研究。然而，他们带着偏见进行调查，认为欧洲人和欧洲社会在生物学方面和文化方面都优于其他所有人，认为殖民地的人民未开化，需要"文明的教化"。这种现象助推了西欧帝国主义在 19 世纪和 20 世纪初期的崛起，因为当时的执政者利用这些理论来为其殖民帝国的扩张辩护。

20 世纪早期，殖民政府指派人类学家对殖民地进行研究，包括对一些具体问题的调查，比如殖民地人民对税收等殖民政策的反应。[10] 这再一次表明，这种"科学"的研究方法是为某一特定目标服务的，并非客观的调查。

1960 年，在联合国通过《给予殖民地国家和人民独立宣言》之后，许多殖民地国家获得独立。人们开始怀疑人类学家参与了殖民主义，并对该领域有何意义、是否道德等提出了质询。[11] 格尔茨正是在这样的背景下进行自己的人类学研究。

---

1. 高等研究学院："克利福德·格尔茨（1926—2006）"，登录日期 2015 年 12 月 8 日，https://www.ias.edu/news/press-releases/2009-49。

2. 阿兰姆·延戈扬："克利福德·格尔茨、文化肖像与东南亚"，《亚洲研究期刊》第 68 卷，2009 年 11 月第 4 期，第 1215—1217 页。

3. 安德鲁·亚罗："克利福德·格尔茨，文化人类学家，80 岁辞世"，《纽约时报》，2006 年 11 月 1 日，登录日期 2015 年 12 月 8 日，http://www.nytimes.com/2006/11/01/obituaries/01geertz.html?pagewanted=print&_r=0。

4. 高等研究学院："格尔茨"。

5. 克利福德·格尔茨："通行与事故：一生为学"，载《烛幽之光：哲学问题的人类学省思》，克利福德·格尔茨，普林斯顿：普林斯顿大学出版社，2000 年，第 7 页。

6. 克利福德·格尔茨：《文化的解释》，第 2 版，纽约：基础书局，2000 年，第 89 页。

7. 高等研究学院："格尔茨"。

8. 参见克利福德·格尔茨：《爪哇的宗教》，格伦科：自由出版社，1960 年；《巴厘的人物、时间与行为：一则文化分析》，纽黑文：耶鲁大学东南亚研究，1966 年；《地方性知识：阐释人类学论文集》，纽约：基础书局，1983 年；《论著与生活：作为作者的人类学家》，斯坦福：斯坦福大学出版社，1988 年。

9. 高等研究学院："格尔茨"。

10. 关于殖民人类学的评论史可参见黛安·刘易斯："人类学与殖民主义"，《现代人类学》第 14 卷，1973 年 12 月第 5 期，第 581—602 页。

11. 刘易斯："人类学与殖民主义"，第 581 页。

2 学术背景

要点 &

- 人类学主要对人类的文化进行研究。

- 1871 年，英国人类学家爱德华·伯内特·泰勒爵士*出版了其名作《原始文化》，为文化人类学奠定了基础。[1]

- 与先期的研究者一样，格尔茨相信人类学作为一门学科，依旧重要。但是与以往的学者不同的是，他认为，人类学家对文化的解释，应该基于文化自身的视角，而不应基于外部的视角。

著作语境

克利福德·格尔茨在撰写《文化的解释》(1973)时，涌现出了一批新一代学者。他们认为人类学家应该基于那些生活在某一文化中的人们的视角来研究其文化。在此之前，殖民地的人类学家是"从外部客观地"进行文化研究。他们认为，惟有欧洲殖民者才具备科学能力去辨别一个民族的文化。[2] 格尔茨正是在人类学家开始挑战这些殖民主义实践和观点的时候写这本书的。

为获得对文化的"内在"理解，这些新一代的人类学家将自己置身于研究对象中。学者们将这种方法称为参与者观察*。这些参与观察的人类学家仔细记录了关于人们的文化和共同生活的每一个细节，并试图解释它们的含义。学者们将这一过程以及形成的报告称为民族志*。直到今天，人类学家仍在使用民族志来研究文化现象。

在《文化的解释》中，格尔茨提出了一种特殊的民族志研究方法。这种方法基于他对文化的概念化，认为文化是具有特定意义的象征和象征性仪式的集合。格尔茨独特的理解和研究文化的方法使得人类学摆脱了殖民传统，自成一门学科。

《文化的解释》还帮助界定了人类学的一个分支学科——文化人类学。文化人类学通常指在精神上具有整体性 * 的民族志作品（即这些作品旨在为一个民族的文化、习俗和社会实践提供一种全面、综合的观点）。《文化的解释》推动了 20 世纪美国现代文化人类学的兴起。在 20 世纪 60 年代，它被称为象征或解释人类学运动。

> "《文化的解释》中的所有文章，有时是直接提出，更多的是通过具体的分析来得出一种缩小范畴的、特殊化的，也正是我所设想的理论上更有力的文化概念来取代 E. B. 泰勒著名的'最复杂的整体'的概念。我并不是否定他提出的这一概念的创新力，但在我看来，这一概念所掩盖的远甚于它所揭示的。"
>
> —— 克利福德·格尔茨：《文化的解释》

学科概览

《文化的解释》问世前，关于文化的定义，人类学家们一直沿用英国人类学家爱德华·伯内特·泰勒的文化概念。1871 年，泰勒将文化定义为"一个复杂的整体，包括知识、信仰、艺术、道德、法律、风俗以及人类在社会里习得的一切能力和习惯"。[3] 这个定义奠定了人类学中现代文化概念的基础。

在 20 世纪二三十年代，出生于德国的美国人类学家弗朗茨·博厄斯 * 深刻影响了美国人类学学科。博厄斯认为，人类学家应该对特定文化进行深入研究。他确信，每个社会都是其独特历史轨迹的整体表征。这种理论方法被称为"历史特殊主义"*。

与此同时，波兰的布罗尼斯拉夫·马林诺夫斯基*和英国的阿尔弗雷德·拉德克利夫－布朗*已成为现代欧洲人类学的主要代表人物。他们研究文化的方式在于分析文化习俗是如何保证社会功能发挥作用的。因此，他们的理论方法被称为功能主义*。以功能主义研究考察青少年的入会仪式为例子：在功能主义看来，入会仪式是进入成年的仪式，因此，这些仪式的独特性特征在特定社会中发挥了这种作用。

20世纪50年代，颇有影响力的法国人类学家克劳德·列维－斯特劳斯*提出了一种称为结构主义*的理论和方法论。结构主义关注的是系统诸要素之间的对立关系。例如，列维－斯特劳斯认为，大多数流行的文化模式——如明显存在于语言、仪式和神话中的文化模式——可以在一系列相互对立的概念中进行排列，例如黑与白、雄与雌、昼与夜。

格尔茨否定了博厄斯的文化理论。他发现，博厄斯的理论过于宽泛——涵盖了太多的领域——而且过于普遍，因为它根植于泰勒对文化的定义，适用于所有人、所有地域。格尔茨称之为"概念的泥沼"。[4] 他也从未完全接受过欧洲人类学家关于"文化实践为特定功能服务"的主张。格尔茨同意列维－斯特劳斯关于象征和象征性行为的重要性的观点，但不赞同列维－斯特劳斯研究这些象征和象征性行为时所采用的方法。与列维－斯特劳斯相反，格尔茨认为，象征——而不是它们的对立关系——能够解释社会情境。他认为，象征的意义不是来自于彼此之间的关系，而是取决于这些象征在人们生活中所起的作用。

学术渊源

格尔茨在马萨诸塞州坎布里奇的哈佛大学攻读博士学位，当时，学校刚刚建立了一个跨学科的社会关系学院。哈佛的学习对格尔茨的学术发展产生了极大影响。这种影响在他的《文化的解释》一书中表现得十分明显。格尔茨很早就意识到，从社会科学、艺术和人文学科（如语言、哲学、社会学、历史和文学）等不同学科中所获得的见解，可以帮助解释和分析人类学中的现象。因此，他利用所有这些学科来研究符号所蕴含的意义。[5]

在哈佛大学，格尔茨师从人类学家克莱德·克拉克洪，并在他的引导下开始研究文化人类学。格尔茨终身致力于象征和象征性行为及其在体现意义模式中的作用的研究，对此，克拉克洪功不可没。社会学家塔尔科特·帕森斯也为格尔茨在哈佛大学的发展发挥了重要作用：帕森斯向格尔茨推荐了德国社会学家马克斯·韦伯[*]的著作。英国语言哲学家吉尔伯特·赖尔[*]对格尔茨也产生了影响。赖尔认为，思维的运作方式与身体的行为没有什么不同。换言之，心理词汇只是描述行动的另一种方式。学者们认为韦伯是社会学的三大奠基人之一，另外两位是法国思想家埃米尔·杜尔凯姆[*]和德国政治哲学家卡尔·马克思[*]。韦伯的社会理论为格尔茨的意义解释方法提供了理论依据。格尔茨采用了韦伯的观点，认为学者要想解释人们的行为，首先要理解个人对这些行为赋予的意义。

1. 参见爱德华·伯内特·泰勒:《原始文化:神话、哲学、宗教、语言、艺术与习俗发展之研究》,第 2 卷,伦敦:约翰·默里出版社,1871 年。

2. 高等研究学院:"克利福德·格尔茨(1926-2006)",登录日期 2015 年 12 月 8 日,https://www.ias.edu/news/press-releases/2009-49。

3. 琼·利奥波德:《比较与进化视角下的文化研究:E. B. 泰勒与原始文化的创造》,柏林:迪特里希·赖默尔出版社,1980 年。

4. 克利福德·格尔茨:《文化的解释》,第 2 版,纽约:基础书局,2000 年,第 4 页。

5. 克利福德·格尔茨:"通行与事故:一生为学",载《烛幽之光:哲学问题的人类学省思》,克利福德·格尔茨,普林斯顿:普林斯顿大学出版社,2000 年,第 7 页。

3 主导命题

要点 🔑

- 格尔茨《文化的解释》一书重新界定了文化和人类学的任务。

- 在格尔茨撰写文章时，多数人类学家认为文化具有普遍性，存在于社会结构中。

- 格尔茨大幅度修正了主流争论的理论，缩小了占主导地位的文化概念的内涵。

核心问题

在《文化的解释》（1973）一书中，克利福德·格尔茨试图解决人类学需要对文化概念进行重新界定的问题。通过重新界定，他希望重申人类学作为一门学科的必要性。格尔茨著述的《文化的解释》展示了一种新的文化概念，认为"（文化是）使用各种象征来表达的一套世代相传的概念体系，人们凭借这套体系可以交流、延续和发展他们有关生活的知识和对待生活的态度。"[1] 换言之，格尔茨想把文化概念缩小为一种意义模式，这种意义模式表现为象征和象征性行为。

象征（比如一只白鸽）和象征性动作（比如一个微笑）均表达一定的思想，代表的意义与物体或姿势的字面意义大不相同，含义更深。例如，白鸽象征着和平，微笑可能象征着对接受微笑者的情感。象征使用的场合不同，其代表的意义也会改变。例如，链子既可以象征"联合"，也可以代表"监禁"。因此，某一个动作或一件物品的象征意义取决于使用它的时间、地点和方式，以及它的"读者"。

格尔茨认为，特别重要的象征或仪式是对整个文化的反映。例如，格尔茨解释了他如何通过观察当地斗鸡的仪式和就斗鸡进行的赌博的过程来了解印度尼西亚巴厘岛文化。他写道，巴厘男人将雄鸡视为"理想化的自我"，将斗鸡视为同社会竞争一样激烈的竞技场。格尔茨认为，这些象征蕴含的意义，取决于它们在人们生活中的作用。这就是为什么我们必须将其作为一种现象来进行研究的原因。他认为人类学家的主要任务应该是揭示并解释象征的意义。

> "下面的所有文章，均从不同的角度，用不同的方法，致力于复原文化概念的本来面目，从而实际上确保了文化概念继续保持重要性，而不是削弱文化概念。"
>
> —— 克利福德·格尔茨：《文化的解释》

参与者

与格尔茨同时代的人类学家中几乎没人赞同他对文化的定义。与格尔茨同时代的罗杰·基辛*，一位颇具影响力的美国文化人类学家，在20世纪60年代总结了"重新思考文化"的四种不同理论。[2]

第一种理论认为文化是相互关联的各个部分，构成一个总体结构。这一理论最著名的拥护者是法国学者克劳德·列维－斯特劳斯，他认为，许多常见的文化模式都源于思维的基本结构。他认为人类的思维模式形成了组成我们世界观的文化范畴。比如，他认为人的大脑有一种将对立的概念（如亮与暗、雌和雄）进行分类的先天倾向。在他看来，这些基本的概念模式构成了文化的基础。这种极受欢迎的结构主义理论，主导着当时人类学的学术研究。

第二种是美国学者马歇尔·萨林斯*和罗伊·拉帕波特*提出的生态理论，将文化视为适应性系统。适应性系统是指一组相互关联的部分，形成一个统一的整体，从而回应和适应环境的变化。适应性系统的例子包括自然生态系统或人类社区。生态人类学*家研究人类与其生物物理环境之间的关系，探究人们是如何适应周围环境以维持自身的生存。

当时重新思考文化的第三种理论认为，文化是认知系统（即与人们的心理知识相关）。查尔斯·弗雷克*和詹姆斯·斯普拉德利*等学者试图将文化视为共享知识的模式。认知人类学*主要研究不同群体的人们了解什么样的知识，以及这些知识是如何塑造他们认识周围的世界，并与这个世界建立关联。

重新定义文化概念的第四种理论是将文化视为象征系统的集合。这一理论的创始人主要包括欧洲的路易·杜蒙*和维克托·特纳*、美国的克利福德·格尔茨和大卫·施耐德*。象征人类学家研究仪式和象征的特定文化含义，通常对一种特别重要的仪式或象征的含义进行探索，旨在揭示这种仪式或象征是如何反映整个文化的。

当时的论战

格尔茨认为，文化语境会影响象征的具体含义。他对"特定的、视情境而定的、具体的"尤为关注，与美国人类学家弗朗茨·博厄斯强调"特定的文化"不谋而合。[3] 几十年前，博厄斯就主张人类学家应该对特定的文化及其历史进行研究，这一主张与当时盛行的"人类学家应该试图了解全人类的进化"的观点形成鲜明对比。

欧洲人类学家布罗尼斯拉夫·马林诺夫斯基和阿尔弗雷德·拉德克利夫-布朗主张社会结构与其功能之间具有相关性，格尔茨承认这一观点。但是，他又把文化与社会结构区别开来。在格尔茨看来，社会结构涵盖了人与人之间的政治、经济和社会关系，而文化反映了人们的生活环境。

在《文化的解释》一书中，格尔茨直截了当地反驳了当时文化人类学中的重要人物之一、结构主义思想家克劳德·列维-斯特劳斯的观点。格尔茨指责列维-斯特劳斯过度简化复杂的文化，结果导致文化最小化、模糊化、扭曲化。格尔茨认为结构主义方法只关注图式关系，而在他看来，象征的意义不是来自于它们彼此之间的关系，而是来自这些象征在人们生活中所起的作用。格尔茨强烈反对结构主义对文化共性的关注，即这些文化共性适用于任何地方或任何情况。他认为，列维-斯特劳斯"让历史变得毫无意义，将情感贬低为理智的影子，用我们所有人内在的野性思维来取代特定的丛林中特定的野蛮人所特有的思维。"[4]

---

1. 克利福德·格尔茨：《文化的解释》，第 2 版，纽约：基础书局，2000 年，第 89 页。
2. 罗杰·基辛："文化理论"，《人类学年度评论》第 3 卷，1974 年，第 73 页。
3. 格尔茨：《文化的解释》，第 89 页。
4. 格尔茨：《文化的解释》，第 355 页。

4 作者贡献

要点 ⚷━━

- 在格尔茨看来，文化应该狭义地定义为在公共生活中由象征性行为表现出来的、并通过深描*方式来解释的意义。深描是指对人类行为的描述要联系其所处的语境，只有这样，人类行为的意义才能为他人所理解。
- 《文化的解释》提倡对文化加以解释的方法来理解文化，为人类学指明了一个新的方向。
- 格尔茨在整合社会学理论和语言哲学的基础上重新思考文化。

作者目标

克利福德·格尔茨耗时 15 年，完成了《文化的解释》一书中的所有文章。其中大部分文章在此书出版之前已经单独发表。在 20 世纪 70 年代早期，当格尔茨着手将其汇编出版时，他已发现，"文化再现"是他作为人类学家"最持久的兴趣"。[1]他主要的目的是提出"何为文化，文化在社会生活中起怎样的作用，以及应该如何正确地进行文化研究"。[2]因此，格尔茨只收录了那些直接探讨文化概念的文章，并将这些文章"按逻辑顺序而非按时间顺序进行排列"。[3]

在这本书的引言中，格尔茨概述了他的总体立场，并为全书搭建了一个总体框架。[4]格尔茨认为，人类学家只有"将研究对象置于其所处的日常系统中"，在"不削弱其特殊性的情况下，展示其常态"，才能理解一个民族的文化。[5]格尔茨建议通过观察象征和象征性行为来做到这一点——在他看来,这些事物代表着一种文化。他探讨了斗鸡这样的象征性行为对该文化中的人意味着什么——一种"共同的意义"。通过这种方法,他相信人类学家可以展示这些知识"对它所处的社会以及更广泛的社会生活能够揭示什么"。[6]

例如,格尔茨发现,印度尼西亚巴厘岛的斗鸡不仅仅是娱乐:斗鸡这一行为不能仅仅通过其表面目的来解释。相反,在巴厘岛,斗鸡是一种象征性行为:公鸡具有隐喻意义,是其所有者的象征。巴厘岛男人参与斗鸡不是为了奖金,而是在斗鸡中取胜能够彰显其社会地位。

巴厘岛人认为宇宙是一个庞大的等级体系,因此他们依然沉迷于社会地位。这种等级体系源于波利尼西亚的头衔和印度教的种姓(社会阶级),将动物和恶魔置于最底层,将国王和神灵放在顶端,而普通人位于这两个极端之间。这种复杂的等级排列为每个人分配了固定的地位。这样庞大的等级体系便构成了巴厘岛社会的道德支柱。斗鸡展示(并实现)了巴厘岛人对自身及其社会环境的认识。

> "在人类学,或者至少是在社会人类学中,实践者所做的是民族志。惟有理解民族志是什么,或者更确切地说,理解民族志研究什么,我们才能开始理解作为一种知识形式的人类学分析是什么。"
>
> —— 克利福德·格尔茨:《文化的解释》

研究方法

格尔茨把这本书的 15 篇文章分成 5 个部分,为他研究文化的新方法搭建了框架，这也使他系统地确立了他对解释人类学的论点。

在《文化的解释》前两部分中，格尔茨借鉴了哲学、文学理论和社会学。他颇有分寸地建立了他的理论基础，将文化定义为一系列象征或象征性行为所体现的意义。在该书第三和第四部分中，格尔茨考察了两种特定的文化体系：宗教和意识形态。

在这两部分中，格尔茨关注的重点"从普遍意义上的文化如何为人类有机体提供有序的形式——缺少这些有序形式，人类就无法思考和感觉——转向特定的文化如何以其特定的象征形式为其成员提供特定的意义和秩序体系，使其在这种特定的文化中生活。"[7] 例如，格尔茨认为宗教是一种特定的文化体系，由一系列特定的符号组成。这些符号勾勒出存在的一般顺序或者说"真正的真实"。对格尔茨而言，宗教象征是对"真正的真实"概念化的载体。要想研究这些象征，必须多加关注宗教。

格尔茨对体现特定文化体系的象征进行了详细描述。他还记录了这些象征所激发的行为和情绪，以及这些象征在特定语境中的意义。这种对象征的详细描述就是格尔茨所指的深描，是格尔茨自己研究民族志时使用的方法。通过深描，他可以清楚地阐明一组特定象征所蕴含的意义模式。

在《文化的解释》的第五部分和最后一部分中，格尔茨运用他的方法对巴厘岛的文化形态进行了解释。

格尔茨应用深描的方法对文化体系进行描述，对当时占主导地位的实证主义*研究传统提出了挑战。在人类学中，实证主义的理论认为，社会事实是独立于人而存在的对象，是人们赋予它们的意义，以及观察者所采取的与它们相关的行为。实证主义的解释创造了与这些对象有关的命题，这些都可以通过观察或实验来验证或证明。

时代贡献

格尔茨将德国社会学家马克斯·韦伯开创的解释方法引入到人类学领域。韦伯关于维斯特恩（Verstehen）*的概念强调了个人对自己的行为所赋予的意义的重要性。德语单词 Verstehen 是指"深入理解"。研究人员通过从他人的角度来对个人进行深入理解，为此，他们可以采访个人和小团体，以及直接体验他们的文化。通过这种方法，人类学家能够更好地理解和解释文化中的意义。前几代人类学家认为，一套法则和价值观可以适用于人类的所有经历。

韦伯的维斯特恩概念为格尔茨试图从文化主体的主观角度（即基于他们的观点，根据他们的特定背景）来理解文化意义提供了重要启示。[8] 格尔茨采用了韦伯的维斯特恩概念，将解释主义引入了当代人类学。解释主义认为，如果我们不了解人们是如何看待某种境况的，我们就无法理解人们对这种情况的反应。格尔茨的原创理论使《文化的解释》成为 20 世纪 60 年代解释人类学运动的"首席发言人"。[9]

---

1. 克利福德·格尔茨：《文化的解释》，第 2 版，纽约：基础书局，2000 年，第 v 页。
2. 格尔茨：《文化的解释》，第 vii 页。
3. 格尔茨：《文化的解释》，第 viii, ix 页。
4. 格尔茨：《文化的解释》，第 ix 页。
5. 格尔茨：《文化的解释》，第 14 页。
6. 格尔茨：《文化的解释》，第 26—27 页。

7. 雪莉·奥特纳："克利福德·格尔茨（1926—2006）",《美国人类学家》第 109 卷，2007 年第 4 期，第 787 页。

8. 奥特纳："克利福德·格尔茨（1926—2006）"，第 787 页。

9. 理查德·施韦德："克利福德·格尔茨的果断与不决",《通识》第 13 卷，2007 年春秋刊第 2—3 期，第 191—205 页。

第二部分：学术思想

5 思想主脉

要点 ⑧━

- 《文化的解释》的核心主题包括文化的本质、文化的运作方式以及学者应该如何研究文化。

- 该书首先认为文化存在于象征性行为中。象征性行为代表抽象的观念，必须在它们特定的社会背景下加以解释。

- 格尔茨在他的主要论点中剖析了文化的主要元素。

核心主题

在《文化的解释》（1973）一书中，克利福德·格尔茨主张将文化理解为一个具有共同意义的系统，即同一社会成员所持有的集体理解。格尔茨提出，每个社会都有其象征和象征性行为，这些代表了社会共同意义的主要原则。例如，每个国家都有一面象征着这个国家的国旗。这些象征和象征性行为作为能指或载体，代表了某一特定文化的共同意义。格尔茨总结道，人类学家通过解读诸如神话和仪式等特别重要的象征和象征性行为来深入了解一种文化。这种解读揭示了象征所代表的意义。

格尔茨认为，在解读象征和象征性行为的意义时，人类学家应该像当地人一样在他们特定的社会背景下解读意义。然后，人类学家需要翻译并向外界解释这些意义。格尔茨解释说，人类学家只有全心投入他们所研究的文化才能做到这一点。全心投入让人类学家能够详细描述他们观察到的日常生活和实践，并确定后者的社会基础和重要性。格尔茨将这种特定的民族志方法称为"深描"。这个术语是他从英国哲学家吉尔伯特·赖尔的著作中借用而来的。

格尔茨认为，深描是一种解释行为、言语和物体的文化语境以及人们赋予它们的意义的方式。深描提供了足够的语境，让文化之外的人能够理解这种行为。相比之下，浅描所陈述的事实就没有了这种含义或重要性。在《文化的解释》中，格尔茨提出人类学家应该考虑的主要任务是提供深描并将其解释给外界。[1]

> "我主张的文化概念本质上是一个符号学的概念，下列各文将试图阐明它的效用。我与马克斯·韦伯一样，认为人是一种悬挂在由他自己编织的意义之网中的动物，我把文化看作这些网络，因此，对文化的分析不是一门寻求规律的实验科学，而是一门探索意义的解释性科学。"
>
> —— 克利福德·格尔茨:《文化的解释》

思想探究

格尔茨声称，"人类是悬挂在由他自己编织的意义之网中的动物，我把文化看作这些网。"他解释说，人们塑造他们的行为模式，并赋予他们的生活方式以意义和重要性。[2] 这些意义或者说这些意义之网是一群人的集体财产——我们称之为"文化"。

人们依靠这些共同的意义来维持他们的社会生活。他们在公共象征和象征性行为中体现了这些共同的意义，这样文化内的人可以学习和分享它们，而文化外的人可以识别它们。象征和象征性行为也传递意义，传达编码信息，帮助人们确定他们应该如何看待自己和他人，以及他们应该如何感知这个世界。

通过关注象征和象征性行为在捕捉、承载和传递我们称之为"文化"的共有意义网中的核心作用，格尔茨提出了符号学*范畴的文化概念———一种植根于符号和象征的文化概念，集中体现了符号和象征所代表的抽象思想。格尔茨的符号学文化观认为，象征的意义不是一成不变的，它可以根据行为人的背景和动机而变化。

　　鉴于此，格尔茨认为，人类学家必须阐明"隐含的或未阐明的预设、内涵或意义，因为这些预设、内涵或意义有助于某种特定语境下的某种文化成员或群体成员理解这样或那样的行为、实践、对象或声音模式。"[3]换言之，人类学家解开了象征或象征性行为呈现在特定语境中的意义之网，然后将其翻译并传达给外界。

　　在格尔茨看来，这项任务很像是试图阅读一整套文本，人类学家们努力"越过（这些文本）真正所有者的肩膀去解读它们"。[4]对他而言，对"文化文本"进行解读是深描的精髓。英国语言哲学家吉尔伯特·赖尔指出了在具体情景下的"深描"和没有上下文的"浅描"之间的区别。[5]

　　赖尔以人"快速抽动右眼皮"即眨眼的物理动作为例子加以说明。出现这种情况的人，可能患有无法控制的抽搐；也可能他或她故意这样做，以便与其他人交流，例如吸引注意力；也可能眨眼的人是为了取笑神经抽搐的人。这一切都取决于眨眼的人的具体情境和意图。这意味着沟通、描述和解释不能明确分开。除了对人的动作和行为的最琐碎的描述之外，所有的描述都涉及对人们为何会按照自己的方式行事、这样做想要达到何种目的等方面进行解释、预测和解读。格尔茨认为，实质上我们必须关注人们行为的全部含义，这样我们才能确定我们理解了这些行为。

语言表述

　　格尔茨系统地阐述了他的论点，他在书中"有时是直接提出，更多的是通过具体的分析来得出一种缩小范畴的、特殊化的以及……理论上更有力的文化概念。"[6] 为此，《文化的解释》中的文章首先定义了文化，然后研究了两种特定的文化体系，最后运用格尔茨的深描法解读了一种特殊的仪式。

尽管作者努力使之系统化，评论家们还是觉得这本书很复杂，有些难懂。格尔茨的写作风格生动而富有诗意，但并未带来任何帮助。该书文体独特，没有采用简单的解释，而是通过隐喻和轶事等手段来表达其观点。事实上，一位评论家将格尔茨比作"民族志的简·奥斯汀*"（19 世纪英国小说家）。[7] 美国哲学家理查德·罗蒂*将格尔茨的作品描述为"关于思维过程的自觉展示和评论"。[8]

因此，普通读者经常误解和曲解《文化的解释》。格尔茨的学生雪莉·奥特纳注意到，一篇讣告称格尔茨的思想"模糊不清"，并哀叹他将人类学"变成了一种蹩脚和混乱的文学研究"。[9]

---

1. 理查德·施韦德："克利福德·格尔茨"，《美国哲学学会会刊》第 154 卷，2010 年 3 月第 1 期，第 90 页。
2. 克利福德·格尔茨：《文化的解释》，第 2 版，纽约：基础书局，2000 年，第 5 页。
3. 格尔茨：《文化的解释》，第 10 页。
4. 格尔茨：《文化的解释》，第 452 页。
5. 吉尔伯特·赖尔：《心的概念》，芝加哥：芝加哥大学出版社，1949 年。
6. 格尔茨：《文化的解释》，第 viii 页。
7. 罗纳托·罗萨尔多："格尔茨的礼物"，《通识》第 13 卷，2007 年第 2—3 期，第 208 页。

8. 理查德·施韦德和拜伦·古德:《同事眼中的克利福德·格尔茨》,芝加哥:芝加哥大学出版社,2005年,第50页。

9. 雪莉·奥特纳:"克利福德·格尔茨(1926—2006)",《美国人类学家》第109卷,2007年第4期,第788页。

6 思想支脉

要点 🗝️

- 格尔茨的两条思想支脉包括他对宗教和意识形态作为文化体系的解释。

- 格尔茨的"宗教和意识形态是特定的意义体系"的理论，远远领先于他所处的时代。

- 当今社会在宗教和意识形态方面的分歧越来越大，格尔茨的理论对当前的争论仍具有重要的借鉴意义。

其他思想

克利福德·格尔茨的《文化的解释》包含了两条重要的思想支脉，即宗教和意识形态这两个特定的"意义体系"。格尔茨借此来阐述他的核心论点。

格尔茨展示了宗教和意识形态是如何为人们提供特定的意义体系，并帮助人们规划生活的。[1] 他提出，宗教是一种文化体系，用于定义什么对人们来说是"真正的真实"；[2] 它是一组符号，通过建立存在的一般顺序，即事物在宇宙和物质层面上的存在方式，在人们心中创造令人信服的和持久的感觉。这些概念以事实为外衣，换言之，它们是以事实呈现出来。通过这种方式，由象征系统所创造的感觉变得极其真实和形象。[3]

格尔茨以同样的方式审视意识形态。他声称，就像宗教一样，意识形态充当"文化象征的有序系统"，为人们明确方向，指引道路。[4] 人们使用意识形态的象征系统来表达对一整套思想的政治信仰；这些思想可能涉及社会分工、机构权力、组织框架和统治精英。格尔茨指出，人们接受一种意识形态的"意义体系"，以缓解他们的紧张。这些紧张可能来自很多方面，如观察他们周围的世界或失去社会和政治方向。意识形态吸引我们的情感欲望，让我们相信有高于生活的可能性。意识形态既是我们希望的表达，也是我们绝望的反映。

格尔茨通过解释 1945 年至 1968 年间从殖民统治中获得政治独立的 66 个国家的意识形态发展来阐明他的论点。他论证了意识形态党派是如何根据特定社会的需要和其历史情况的要求来操纵象征的意义的。

> "审视社会行为的象征性维度——艺术、宗教、意识形态、科学、法律、道德、常识——不是为了逃脱现实生活的困境，寻求六根清净的天国*境界，而是为了投身于这些困境当中去。"
>
> —— 克利福德·格尔茨：《文化的解释》

思想探究

格尔茨认为，在人们生活中"根本没有真正的秩序——没有经验规律，没有情感形式，没有道德凝聚力"的世界里，宗教起着一个安抚人心的主要文化系统的作用。通过这个象征系统，宗教呈现出"这个世界充满了真正秩序的形象，它将解释甚至赞美人们感知到的含糊不清、困惑和悖论。"[5] 换句话说，格尔茨认为宗教的存在是为了安慰人们，并让他们相信一切都有秩序。

为了实现这一点，"宗教象征起着合成一个民族精神气质以及他们的世界观的作用。"[6] 那么，从本质上来说，宗教观点使人们能够感觉到生活理应呈现的面貌（正如宗教所许诺的）与事物的真实状态之间的联系。

格尔茨通过讨论爪哇岛一名突然死亡的男孩的葬礼来说明这一点。这一仪式未能达到产生艾克拉斯 *（接受死亡）、鲁昆 *（群体和谐）等目的。相反，它加剧了社会紧张。格尔茨认为这一丧葬仪式失败主要是由于以下几个原因。

第一，由于当地官员和男孩家庭所属政党之间的冲突，该群体没有遵循通常的伊斯兰程序。第二，为了让葬礼继续进行而做临时修改时，没有就改变葬礼仪式的方式达成集体共识，而是由一个人负责，单方面做出更改。在格尔茨看来，葬礼上发生的冲突，源于群体文化信仰和现实生活中的社会互动之间日益扩大的差距。

格尔茨认为意识形态的作用是"辩护"和"辩解"：它建立并捍卫信仰和价值模式。[7] 在格尔茨看来，意识形态只寻求选择性的问答，只针对狭隘的问题，从而导致它们低估或夸大社会现实。例如，20 世纪三四十年代欧洲普遍存在的反犹太主义 * 思想（对犹太人的敌意）将社会和经济问题归咎于一个敌人：犹太人。格尔茨主张建立一个分析框架，将意识形态视为不同利益集团在持续的权力斗争中使用的武器之外的东西。他指出，"意识形态"一词具有"评价性"的含义，这使得它成为一种对社会、政治和思想疾病的诊断，这些疾病使社会偏离了对现实的理性认识。

在第二次世界大战之后，在被称为冷战 * 的长期全球紧张局势中，以及在许多国家（特别是非洲、亚洲和加勒比地区）殖民时期结束后的政治动荡中，格尔茨察觉到意识形态实际上"是从人们信仰的东西和现在或将来可以被证实为科学正确的东西之间的差异中获得了说服力"。[8] 因此，他指出，社会科学需要发展一种"真正非评估性的意识形态概念"（这种概念并不寻求建立任何意识形态的合理性），能够将社会背景和心理背景考虑进来。[9] 这一主张提供了一种途径，以社会科学家普遍认为有用的方式来定义"意识形态"。

被忽视之处

尽管格尔茨在《文化的解释》中提出了严密而复杂的论点，但是我们并不能认为所有重要的方面都已得到了研究和讨论。在过去的 40 年里，许多学者对这本书的方方面面提出了不同的观点。的确，正如一位评论家所言："批评格尔茨已经成为人类学中一项令人痴迷的研究，几乎成了人类学家的成人礼。"[10]

学者们把注意力集中在许多方面，其中包括：该书认为"文化是进化的内在因素"的观点、关于特定"意义系统"的理论、它的深描方法、它的区域性焦点和民族志、它对重要的现代理论和概念的忽视、它对人类学以外学科的影响、它对社会和道德哲学问题的思考乃至该书的文采。[11]

在当代政治事件、社会问题和历史发展的背景下来重新审视这部著作可能会产生新的、有趣的见解，但是这对我们整体理解《文化的解释》不会产生太大的影响。基于同样的原因，格尔茨完成论文后 10 年直至 1973 年出版，并没有改变任何实质性内容，来改进或更新其论点。当他在 2000 年重新出版这部作品时，整个世界和人类学领域已经发生了很多变化。然而，他仍然没有做出实质性的修改。正如格尔茨自己所言："我当时提出的一些问题已被证明是值得研究的。"[12]

1. 雪莉·奥特纳："克利福德·格尔茨（1926—2006）"，《美国人类学家》第 109 卷，2007 年第 4 期，第 787 页。

2. 克利福德·格尔茨：《文化的解释》，第 2 版，纽约：基础书局，2000 年，第 112 页。

3. 格尔茨：《文化的解释》，第 90 页。

4. 格尔茨：《文化的解释》，第 196 页。

5. 格尔茨：《文化的解释》，第 107—108 页。

6. 格尔茨：《文化的解释》，第 89 页。

7. 格尔茨：《文化的解释》，第 231 页。

8. 格尔茨：《文化的解释》，第 72 页。

9. 格尔茨：《文化的解释》，第 196 页。

10. E. 布鲁纳："《克利福德·格尔茨：他的批评者和追随者》书评，1998 年"，《人类学与人文主义》第 23 卷，1998 年第 2 期，第 216 页。

11. 奥特纳："克利福德·格尔茨（1926—2006）"，第 787 页。

12. 格尔茨：《文化的解释》，第 vi 页。

7 历史成就

要点 🗝

- 格尔茨成功地发表了一部"文化理论专著"。

- 《文化的解释》的出版恰好满足了人类学重新塑造自身学科的需求。

- 在人类学的学科领域内外，在不同的地点、时间和文化中，《文化的解释》都是有价值的。

观点评价

20 世纪 70 年代初，克利福德·格尔茨的出版商请他挑选一套他的论文，并整理成书，这本书就是后来的《文化的解释》。起初，他还不确定自己的意图是什么。格尔茨将他在印度尼西亚几年实地工作的大部分论文称为"经验主义研究"（即基于可通过观察验证的信息的研究）。他最终决定把他所有的此类论文都收集进来，这些论文"直接而明确地阐述了文化的概念"，以及如何研究这一概念。[1] 他想与世界分享他对文化的定义，即意义之网，以及他对研究这些意义之网的解释性方法。

为了做到这一点，他必须解释和翻译文化主体的主观意义和语境含义。格尔茨认为："惟有理解民族志是什么，或者更确切地说，理解民族志是研究什么，我们才能开始理解作为一种知识形式的人类学分析是什么。"[2]（"民族志"是指探索文化现象的研究，记录在书面的实地研究或案例研究中。）在展示他对文化的解释性研究所产生的科学知识的同时，格尔茨也强调人类学作为一门学科的重要性。

公平地说，格尔茨在《文化的解释》中提出的论点已达到了目的。该书呼吁"通过意义的不断产生和转变来理解"人类的处境，这被证明对知识环境的演变至关重要。[3] 它引发了人类学中称为"解释性转向"的学科目标和方法的根本转变。[4] 格尔茨的"文化理论专著"不仅提出了文化的新定义（人类学中的核心、统一的概念，为美国研究实践所采用），而且还成功地确立了以下原则：我们应该通过解释任何特定文化中的人们赋予其社会行为的主观意义来研究文化。

格尔茨的论文集也成功地挑战了当时占主导地位的普遍的、包罗万象的文化观念，它质疑了实证主义方法研究文化的价值，后者认为社会事实独立于人及其意义而存在。它也提供了结构主义和功能主义以外的研究方法——结构主义和功能主义都只关注结构中隐含的意义；功能主义认为社会和文化行为的所有方面都是"有机体的组成部分"，因而，在一个社会的"有机体"中起着重要作用。格尔茨的深描方法不仅对他的民族志方法进行了界定，也对一般文化人类学家的方法进行了界定。

> "某些观念以巨大的力量冲击了知识界。这些观念一下子解决了如此多的基本问题，以至于它们似乎有望解决所有的基本问题，澄清所有的模糊之处。"
>
> —— 克利福德·格尔茨：《文化的解释》

当时的成就

当人类学正努力重塑其学科地位时，《文化的解释》在各大书店亮相。从业者开始质疑和重新思考前几代人提出的文化核心概念。格尔茨的思想塑造了美国文化人类学的新定义。

《文化的解释》一书推动文化人类学成为人类学的一个受到尊重和重视的分支。它将这门学科分别与美国的生物人类学 *（人类进化研究）、语言人类学 *（对语言及其如何代表文化的研究）和考古人类学 *（对人类文化历史轨迹的研究）区别开来，与英国的社会人类学（对社会结构及其在人类文化中的作用的研究）区别开来。它为文化人类学在殖民时期结束后的时代提供了理论基础，并激发了现代文化比较研究（通过研究文化的异同来理解文化的研究）的发展。

作为人类学解释性运动的倡导者，这部著作更对广大知识界产生了直接影响。虽然许多学者仍对格尔茨只强调象征持怀疑态度，但是他们认为《文化的解释》可以作为解释性调查的参考。这是一部开创性的著作，它影响了许多学科的理论和方法。最有影响力的社会科学书籍经常引用它。《文化的解释》被翻译成 20 种语言，使格尔茨成为"一个真正的社会和文化理论巨人"。[5]

局限性

今天，我们正努力应对诸如网络欺凌 * 和全球变暖 * 等社会问题，这是格尔茨 40 年前写作《文化的解释》时无法预见的。这种"局限性"或许是不可避免的。格尔茨在他的"文化专著"中通常是对静态的、小规模的、同质的（内部相似的）和相对孤立的社会进行研究。[6] 相比之下，现代文化是流动的，其特点是缺乏统一性。身份和主体性 *（对我们因身份不同而产生的不同经验的解释）溶解在构成每一种当代文化的意义之网中；男人、女人、穆斯林、佛教徒、吸毒者、禁酒者、同性恋者、异性恋者、双性恋者（仅举几例）在不同程度上促使了这些意义之网的形成。

今天，人们认为自己是多元文化的一部分。他们所认同的文化可能属于他们特定的种族群体、居住的国家、工作的机构、社会阶层、宗教团体或虚拟朋友*——诸如此类。在当今的世界里，文化既不是封闭的，也不是孤立的，任何人都可以像他或她所希望的那样成为任何特定文化的一部分。人们在任何时候都已经对一系列文化（即意义系统）中不同意义片段的集合进行了内在化。[7]这使得"文化"的定义比格尔茨写这部著作时更加难以界定。

---

1. 克利福德·格尔茨：《文化的解释》，第 2 版，纽约：基础书局，2000 年，第 vii 页。

2. 格尔茨：《文化的解释》，第 5—6 页。

3. 雪莉·奥特纳："克利福德·格尔茨（1926—2006）"，《美国人类学家》第 109 卷，2007 年第 4 期，第 787 页。

4. 雪莉·奥特纳："专题：'文化'的命运：格尔茨及其他"，《再现》第 59 卷，1997 年，第 6 页。

5. 杰弗里·亚历山大等编：《解释克利福德·格尔茨：社会科学中的文化调查》，纽约：帕尔格雷夫·麦克米伦出版社，2011 年，第 xiii 页。

6. 格尔茨：《文化的解释》，第 viii 页。

7. 戴维·克朗菲尔德等编：《认知人类学指南》，新加坡：布莱克威尔出版有限公司，2011 年。

8 著作地位

要点 &—

- 格尔茨一生的著述重点是文化的再现 *（即文化的翻译）。

- 《文化的解释》被认为是一部杰作，成为格尔茨最著名的出版物。

- 《文化的解释》使格尔茨成为人类学解释性运动或象征性运动的奠基人之一。

定位

在克利福德·格尔茨收集他的论文并以《文化的解释》一书发表之前，他曾在芝加哥大学担任人类学教授长达 10 年。在 1960 年到 1970 年间，格尔茨将研究重点放在印度尼西亚的爪哇岛和巴厘岛上，出版了三本书：《爪哇的宗教》（1960）、《农业内化》（1963）和《小贩与王子》（1963）。[1]20 世纪 60 年代，格尔茨在摩洛哥从事研究，出版了大量著作，其中一本名为《伊斯兰观察》（1968），书中他对印度尼西亚和摩洛哥进行了比较研究。[2]

格尔茨在普林斯顿大学高等研究学院担任社会科学教授之后出版了《文化的解释》。这本书收录了格尔茨在 20 世纪 60 年代单独发表的一些论文。格尔茨故意选择不出版一本"他职业生涯的回顾或自传"。[3] 相反，他希望在工作中找到一条主线。当他梳理他的论文时，他认为"文化的再现（解释）"是他"作为人类学家最持久的兴趣"。[4]

尽管多年来格尔茨的学术立场略有改变，但他克制住了将他"改变后的观点写回早期作品中"的诱惑，[5] 并且没有触及论文的中心论点。《文化的解释》最初出版于 1973 年，当该书于 2000 年重新发行时，格尔茨在原版中添加的唯一实质性内容是一篇导论。这篇导论概述了他的总体立场，并为这本论文集提供了一个总体框架。[6]

> "不管格尔茨是受人尊敬还是受到唾骂，所有从事文化研究的人都应该熟悉他的作品，如同所有的精神分析学家都必须与弗洛伊德[*]打交道，所有社会批判理论家都必须与马克思打交道，所有结构主义者都必须与索绪尔[*]打交道一样。"
>
> —— 杰弗里·亚历山大等：
> 《解释克利福德·格尔茨：社会科学中的文化调查》

整合

《文化的解释》成为格尔茨最著名的出版作品，使他成为解释性运动或象征性运动的创始人之一。1974 年，他编辑了《神话、符号和文化》选集，进一步巩固了这一声誉。[7]该选集收录了一些重要的人类学家关于象征人类学[*]的论文。同期，格尔茨还发表了民族志研究著作，如《巴厘岛的亲属关系》（1975）和与希尔德雷德·格尔茨、劳伦斯·罗森合著的《摩洛哥社会的意义和秩序》（1979）。[8]

从 20 世纪 80 年代起，格尔茨开始在《纽约书评》发表理论文章和评论。在此期间，他写的书多为论文集，包括《地方性知识》（1983）、《烛幽之光》（2000）和《斯人斯世》（2010 年去世后出版）。[9]他还出版了一本关于民族志方法的短论文集，书名为《论著与生活》（1988），以及自传《追寻真实》（1995）。[10]

虽然我们可以肯定地认为格尔茨的整体著作清晰连贯，但他的观点是在他漫长的职业生涯中逐渐形成的。批评家认为，他的学术之旅呈现出三大趋势。[11] 首先，格尔茨越来越相信"知识不是普遍的"。相反，他认定特定见解只有特定的一群人才会认同。其次，格尔茨不再担心功能主义（粗略地说，就是通过考虑文化各个部分所提供的有用"功能"来解释文化），而是越来越关注用符号学的术语（即通过解释性象征和语言）来研究文化的必要性。第三，格尔茨总是把他的方法建立在离散的、具体的"文化肖像"上。但对他来说，似乎有必要"从'文化'（cultures，小写、复数）而不是'文化'（Culture，大写、单数）的角度来思考"。[12]

意义

格尔茨的整体研究影响了许多学科的学者。他对人类学、历史学、社会学、宗教研究和文化研究领域的理论和方法产生了深远的影响。一些人开玩笑说，格尔茨变得如此出名，以至于他产生了自己的"文化体系"。[13] "格尔茨文化"汇总了他作品中的关键术语（如深描）以及经常出现的名言、意象和比喻。批评家们认为，这种具有高辨识度的引述很少见，只见于最有影响力的思想家，如开创性社会学家马克斯·韦伯和具有广泛影响力的政治哲学家卡尔·马克思。[14]

格尔茨的杰作《文化的解释》常常与法国社会学家、人类学家皮埃尔·布尔迪厄*的《区分：判断力的社会批判》和美国社会学家 C. 赖特·米尔斯*的《社会学的想象力》一同被列入最有影响力的科学著作。[15] 此外，《文化的解释》在亚马逊网站上的图书销售排行榜上位列第 8000 名，尽管它 40 多年前出版时，"亚马逊"还只是一条河流。[16]

解释人类学或象征人类学已被证明是人类学学科内外一个流行的、有影响力的学派。正如它 40 年前引领关于文化挪用（文化习惯的习得，通常是由"主导"文化决定）的辩论一样，它仍然是关于全球化（跨大陆边界的文化、经济和政治联系日益密切的趋势）和文化多元化（多种文化在同一社会中共存）的现代辩论的核心。[17]

1. 克利福德·格尔茨：《爪哇的宗教》，格伦科：自由出版社，1960 年；《农业内化：印度尼西亚的生态变迁过程》，洛杉矶：加利福尼亚大学出版社，1963 年；《小贩与王子：印度尼西亚两个城镇的社会变迁与经济现代化》，芝加哥：芝加哥大学出版社，1963 年。

2. 克利福德·格尔茨：《伊斯兰观察：摩洛哥和印度尼西亚的宗教发展》，纽黑文：耶鲁大学出版社，1968 年。

3. 克利福德·格尔茨：《文化的解释》，第 2 版，纽约：基础书局，2000 年，第 viii 页。

4. 格尔茨：《文化的解释》，第 v 页。

5. 格尔茨：《文化的解释》，第 viii 页。

6. 格尔茨：《文化的解释》，第 ix 页。

7. 克利福德·格尔茨：《神话、象征与文化》，纽约：诺顿出版社，1974 年。

8. 克利福德·格尔茨：《巴厘岛的亲属关系》，芝加哥：芝加哥大学出版社，1975 年；克利福德·格尔茨，希尔德雷德·格尔茨，劳伦斯·罗森：《摩洛哥社会的意义与秩序》，纽约：剑桥大学出版社，1979 年。

9. 克利福德·格尔茨：《地方性知识：阐释人类学论文集》，纽约：基础书局，1983 年；《烛幽之光：哲学问题的人类学省思》，普林斯顿：普林斯顿大学出版社，2000 年；《斯人斯世：格尔茨遗文集》，普林斯顿：普林斯顿大学出版社，2010 年。

10. 克利福德·格尔茨：《论著与生活：作为作者的人类学家》，斯坦福：斯坦福大学出版社，1988 年；《追寻事实：两个国家、四个十年、一位人类学家》，马萨诸塞州坎布里奇：哈佛大学出版社，1995 年。

11. 阿兰姆·延戈扬："克利福德·格尔茨、文化肖像与东南亚"，《亚洲研究期刊》第 68 卷，2009 年 11 月第 4 期，第 1215—1216 页。

12. 延戈扬："克利福德·格尔茨"，第 1216 页。

13. 杰弗里·亚历山大等编：《解释克利福德·格尔茨：社会科学中的文化调查》，纽约：帕尔格雷夫·麦克米伦出版社，2011 年，第 xiii—xiv 页。

14. 亚历山大等编：《解释克利福德·格尔茨》，第 xiii—xiv 页。

15. 亚历山大等编：《解释克利福德·格尔茨》，第 xiii—xiv 页；参见皮埃尔·布尔迪厄：《区分：判断力的社会批判》，理查德·尼斯译，马萨诸塞州坎布里奇：哈佛大学出版社，1987 年；C. 赖特·米尔斯：《社会学的想象力》，纽约：牛津大学出版社，1959 年。

16. 亚历山大等编：《解释克利福德·格尔茨》，第 xiv 页。

17. 雪莉·奥特纳："专题：'文化'的命运：格尔茨及其他"，《再现》第 59 卷，1997 年，第 1—14 页。

第三部分：学术影响

9 最初反响

要点 🗝—॥

- 对格尔茨《文化的解释》的主要批评是围绕着作者的主观解释方法（他对文化特性的解释方法，让该文化外的人如他所研究的文化内的人所理解的那样解读文化）、他对象征的关注以及他对权力、冲突、不平等与历史进程的忽视等展开。

- 面对批评，格尔茨只能强调他对社会生活的本质的不同看法，以及他对创造规则来解释人类行为的前景的不同观点。

- 学者们认为，格尔茨的这部著作富有成效，让人们开始运用解释方法来研究文化。

批评

格尔茨出版《文化的解释》一书时，实证主义在人类学研究传统中占据主导地位。实证主义认识论认为，社会事实是独立于人和人赋予这些事实的语境意义而存在的，我们可以通过观察和实验来证实或证明这些事实。实证主义学者认为，格尔茨对文化的研究方法是不科学的。他们认为格尔茨过于依赖解释，从而导致了"不受控制的主观主义"，[1] 换言之，他的发现更多地与他自己的理解有关，而不是与客观的、可证实的"事实"相关。

甚至有些人类学家，明知这种解释方法有诸多益处，仍对《文化的解释》提出了批评。他们认为，格尔茨赋予文化的符号学概念过于狭隘，因为它更多地依赖对符号和象征意义的解读。例如，一些与格尔茨同时代的具有影响力的学者也反对他的象征性方法。如马文·哈里斯 *、罗伊·拉帕波特、马歇尔·萨林斯及安德鲁·P. 瓦伊达 * 等人类学家认为，我们应该把文化理解为人类用来适应在不同环境中生活的非生物手段。他们强调，所有的文化现象的出现都是为了应对地球上生活的实际问题。这些人类学家们批评格尔茨忽视了权力、冲突和不平等。他们也反对格尔茨在政治和道德上的中立态度。[2] 例如，人类学家塔拉尔·阿萨德 * 在研究格尔茨对宗教的定义时，他发现"它忽视了权力的关键层面"，"忽略了产生知识的不同的社会条件"。[3]

学者们持有多种不同观点，他们对格尔茨的开创性著作的解释范围提出了异议。他们指出，"这种解释仅仅基于描述的深度和细节。"换言之，格尔茨是让文化来描述和解释其自身。[4] 例如，历史学家认为，格尔茨对意义体系的解释通常没有考虑到"导致其产生的历史过程"。[5] 塔拉尔·阿萨德也赞同这一说法。他对格尔茨有关宗教的描述给予了批判性评价，并在最后呼吁"根据特定实践和话语存在所必需的历史条件"来研究宗教。[6]

> "的确，批评格尔茨已经成为人类学中一项令人痴迷的研究，几乎成了人类学家的成人礼。"
>
> —— 爱德华·布鲁纳："《克利福德·格尔茨：他的批评者和追随者》书评，1998 年"

回应

格尔茨从未参与过人类学家之间的科学辩论，他也没有花太多的精力为自己的著作进行辩护。他为自己的沉默辩解道，他的主要兴趣是阐明"人类学是一项有意义的项目"。[7]

当受到质疑时，他只想强调他"对社会生活性质的不同看法，以及对有关人类行为的类似法律的解释性陈述的发展前景的不同观点"。[8] 格尔茨并没有将人类文化视为一种权力，人们可以轻而易举地通过识别图式关系和文化共性将社交事件、行为、机构或过程归因于这种权力。[9] 相反，格尔茨将文化理解为特定个体构建意义系统的背景。他强调，"文化的符号学方法的全部意义在于帮助我们进入我们的研究对象所生活的概念世界，这样我们就可以在某种更广泛的意义上与他们交流。"[10]

格尔茨还解释道，大部分决定人类行为的含义范围仍然很狭窄，仅限于特定的地域环境。因此，他认为社会科学的各种归纳不可避免也会受到范围的限制。[11] 在其后来的研究中，格尔茨进一步坚定了他以特殊主义 * 和相对主义 * 的方式研究文化的决心。也就是说，将每一种文化视为一种"个体（单数）"的情况，在这种情况下，其信仰、实践等的有效性或价值不比其他任何文化（尤其是人类学家自身所在的文化）更大或更小。

冲突与共识

虽然很多人类学家对克里福德·格尔茨只强调象征仍存怀疑，但他们认为，这是文化解释方法的一个良好起点，当然还需考虑到文化的其他界定要素，如历史、权力相互作用和社会结构等等。[12]

基于行为者的主观视角来解释意义的重要性，已经成为重要的共识。许多人质疑当时流行的实证主义模型，同意格尔茨的观点，即根据特定情况下行为者的意图和所处的环境来理解意义仍然十分重要。因此，学者们仍然认为，对于那些想要超越实证主义数据收集或者大规模结构理论（这些理论认为，可以通过确定构成文化结构的要素之间的关系来分析文化）的人而言,《文化的解释》是一种强有力的资源。这部著作的命题就是"人类学家必须研究人们如何理解他们周围的世界",学者们从中发现了巨大价值。

尽管受到批评,《文化的解释》仍定义了美国文化人类学学科的核心思想。这似乎是这本书取得共识的有力标志。格尔茨的这部著作将文化人类学从研究人类关系的密切相关的方法（如社会人类学）中区分开来。它为人类学在后殖民时代的存在提供了新的正当性,并促进了现代文化比较研究学科的发展。

1. 雪莉·奥特纳:"专题:'文化'的命运:格尔茨及其他",《再现》第 59 卷,1997 年,第 1—14 页。

2. 爱德华·布鲁纳:"《克利福德·格尔茨:他的批评者和追随者》书评,1998年",《人类学与人文主义》第 23 卷,1998 年第 2 期,第 216 页。

3. 塔拉尔·阿萨德:"宗教人类学概念:对格尔茨的反思",《人类》第 18 卷,1983 年第 2 期,第 237—259 页。

4. 阿兰姆·延戈扬:"克利福德·格尔茨:文化肖像与东南亚",《亚洲研究期刊》第 68 卷,2009 年 11 月第 4 期,第 1217 页。

5. 布鲁纳:"《克利福德·格尔茨:他的批评者和追随者》书评,1998 年",第 216 页。

6. 阿萨德:"宗教人类学概念",第 237 页。

7. 雪莉·奥特纳:"克利福德·格尔茨（1926—2006）",《美国人类学家》第 109 卷,2007 年第 4 期,第 788 页。

8. 理查德·施韦德:"克利福德·格尔茨的果断与不决",《通识》第 13 卷,2007 年春秋刊第 2—3 期,第 197 页。

9. 克利福德·格尔茨：《文化的解释》，第 2 版，纽约：基础书局，2000 年，第 14 页。

10. 格尔茨：《文化的解释》，第 24 页。

11. 施韦德："克利福德·格尔茨的果断与不决"，第 196 页。

12. 布鲁纳："《克利福德·格尔茨：他的批评者和追随者》书评，1998 年"，第 216 页。

10 后续争议

要点 ⚷

- 格尔茨的相对主义方法——他的理论立场，即任何文化的信仰和实践都不能声称具有任何特定的有效性——以及他对另类道德世界（道德的其他系统）的解释吸引了许多学者。

- 许多人认为《文化的解释》推广了一种解释学派的思想。

- 虽然诸多文化人类学家欣赏格尔茨的解释主义，但他们并未将文化视为封闭的和孤立的。因此，他们对格尔茨的方法进行了补充，着眼于更广泛的政治、经济、社会、历史和文化框架，这些框架影响着当地人在他们的文化中赋予意义的方式。

应用与问题

克利福德·格尔茨只强调象征是文化意义的代码，许多学者对此并不认同，但他在《文化的解释》中提出的观点却非常受欢迎。事实上，学者们相信《文化的解释》推广了一种解释学派的思想，同时也影响了诸多不同学科的思维方向。

在借鉴了几个学科的研究目标和方法的基础上，格尔茨在自己的研究中采取了跨学科的方法。他的"文化是一种意义系统"的文化理论，对社会学、宗教研究、心理学、哲学和其他人文科学都具有价值。他的理论还吸引了传播学、地理学、生态学、政治学、比较法学、历史学和文学批评等学科的诸多学者。[1] 他坚持"人的主观世界观和语境世界观具有其独特性"，引起了学术界的关注，同样，他用其解释方法来解释这些世界观也吸引了学者们的关注。另一位著名的美国文化人类学家，理查德·施韦德解释说，《文化的解释》提供了一套"挑衅性的"但又"可移植的"观点，广受各学科学者们的欢迎。

对于很多学者而言，格尔茨的方法不如他的文化多元论重要——文化多元论是他从文化本身的角度思考不同文化的方法，这是他的相对主义方法的核心概念。这也为他对另类道德世界的解释提供了依据（即没有在任何时候都适用于任何人的人类"道德"）。[2]其他学科的思想家普遍采纳了格尔茨的观点："多样性是人类境况所固有的，人性没有普遍的本质。"他们也同意"……把统一性（共同的信仰）看得比多样性重要，忽视、贬低或试图消除差异的那些冲动，都不是一件好事。"[3]

> "结果表明，虽然我们可以超越格尔茨，但我们永远不能把他丢下。"
>
> —— 杰弗里·亚历山大等：
> 《解释克利福德·格尔茨：社会科学中的文化调查》

思想流派

格尔茨以其独特的方法分析文化，为人类学理论和方法指明了新的方向。他使文化分析在本质上具有语境性和解释性。[4]事实上，格尔茨帮助建立了一个新的思想流派，即"解释人类学"或"象征人类学"。他将这种认识人类和社会的方法建立在对主观世界观之网的系统解构的基础之上。[5]解释人类学将学者们的注意力转向了文化和解释问题，这可能是解释人类学最显著的成就。在此之前，人类学家几乎只关注于发展宏大理论。

解释人类学的产生，是受到了当时流行的思想流派如唯物主义 *和马克思主义 * 的直接影响，这些以理解历史和社会为目标的相关流派强调经济和社会阶级等物质因素。（唯物主义认为文化由可观察的行为组成，而马克思主义认为经济和社会阶级等物质因素是历史的主要驱动力。）后来人们所熟知的象征人类学或解释人类学，对随后社会科学中现代思想流派的发展作出了贡献。它还明确提出，要考虑研究人员的个性和亲临现场等因素，这对他（她）所研究的内容影响相当重要。[6]

其他一些重要的研究解释人类学的文化人类学家有：马歇尔·萨林斯、大卫·施耐德、维克多·特纳、玛丽·道格拉斯 *。许多人认为格尔茨和这四位杰出的学者是象征人类学或解释人类学的奠基者。

当代研究

克利福德·格尔茨职业生涯的大部分时间都在偏远地区从事民族志研究。[7]他直接指导的博士生为数不多，但他在普林斯顿高等研究学院任职的 30 年间，通过奖学金、研讨会和午餐谈话的形式影响了数百名社会科学家和历史学家。[8]

那些支持和倡导《文化的解释》的学者，无论来自哪个学科，对格尔茨的解释主义、文化概念、相对主义和特殊主义（他认为对每种文化的理解都应基于它所持有的价值观，而且每种文化都是特定历史和环境背景的产物）以及他的知识交叉渗透的素养和他的文学天赋都给予了赞赏。格尔茨坚持认为"我们对理解的过程要更好地加以理解"，学者们对此表示钦佩。[9]最重要的是，他们赞同格尔茨提出的"从多元化入手研究人类的多样性"的诉求。

在他们自己的工作中，格尔茨的支持者似乎把注意力集中在赋予意义的问题上，而不是文化系统的概念。[10] 这一点，尤其在格尔茨自己的人类学研究领域可以看出来。许多现代民族志学者继续研究不同地方的人们体验生活的不同方式。这类研究学者包括雪莉·奥特纳、莉拉·阿布-卢格霍德＊、乔治·马库斯＊和罗纳托·罗萨尔多＊。然而，他们又与格尔茨不同，并不认为文化是封闭的和孤立的。他们对格尔茨的方法进行了补充，着眼于更广泛的政治、经济、社会、历史和文化框架，这些框架影响着当地人在他们的文化中赋予意义的方式。[11] 格尔茨最引人注目、最直言不讳、最杰出的弟子是文化人类学家雪莉·奥特纳和理查德·施韦德，两人的学术研究都曾获得过奖项。

1. 参见雪莉·奥特纳："专题：'文化'的命运：格尔茨及其他"，《再现》第 59 卷，1997 年，第 1—14 页；理查德·施韦德："克利福德·格尔茨的果断与不决"，《通识》第 13 卷，2007 年春秋刊第 2—3 期，第 191—205 页。
2. 理查德·A. 施韦德和拜伦·古德：《同事眼中的克利福德·格尔茨》，芝加哥：芝加哥大学出版社，2005 年，第 8 页。
3. 奥特纳："专题"，第 1—14 页。
4. 雪莉·奥特纳："克利福德·格尔茨（1926—2006）"，《美国人类学家》第 109 卷，2007 年第 4 期，第 789 页。
5. 奥特纳："克利福德·格尔茨（1926—2006）"，第 787 页。
6. 奥特纳："克利福德·格尔茨（1926—2006）"，第 787 页。
7. 奥特纳："克利福德·格尔茨（1926—2006）"，第 788 页。
8. 奥特纳："克利福德·格尔茨（1926—2006）"，第 787 页。
9. 施韦德和古德：《同事眼中的克利福德·格尔茨》，第 9 页。
10. 奥特纳："专题"，第 1 页。
11. 奥特纳："专题"，第 1—14 页。

11 当代印迹

要点 ⚷

- 《文化的解释》是从事解释研究的人类学家所推崇的著作之一。

- 虽然这些学者已经广泛采纳了格尔茨的"解释性转向",但是学界的普遍共识是,人类学家需要对格尔茨的文化概念进行补充,使其能够适用于现代世界。

- 在格尔茨之后,人类学家需要为日益相互依存、错综复杂且不断变化的世界重新配置文化概念。

地位

克利福德·格尔茨的《文化的解释》首次出版至今已过了 40 年,现在,这部著作已经成为"神圣经典"的一部分,[1] 对于任何对社会科学和人文学科的解释方法感兴趣的人来说,这部著作必不可少。

学者们普遍认为,他们需要通过进一步研究更广泛的政治、经济、社会和历史条件来对格尔茨的文化概念进行补充。即便如此,《文化的解释》的现实意义并没有减弱。[2] 人类学的研究中已经广泛采用了格尔茨的"解释性转向"。直到今天,这种方法仍然被很多文化人类学家和社会人类学家所沿用。历史学家、社会学家、政治科学家以及其他学科的学者收集民族志数据进行项目研究时,通常也使用格尔茨的这种方法。[3] 他们采用这种解释方法对文本意义及具体运用进行梳理和分析。

同样,他们与格尔茨一样,对文化相对主义十分推崇——这就需要从一个社会所持有的价值观的角度来理解这一社会。在全球化时代——即世界各国之间的文化、经济和政治联系日益密切的时代——《文化的解释》可以继续帮助我们理解差异，特别是"不同群体和不同生活方式表现出来的不同的自我、不同的道德、不同的情感、不同的宗教、不同的政治权威、不同的亲属关系、不同的时间观念等等"。[4] 无论是在人类学领域之内还是领域之外，有关《文化的解释》的争论不断，引用也不断。

> "不管'文化'概念有什么缺陷……也要在存在缺陷的情况下坚持研究。"
> —— 雪莉·奥特纳："专题：'文化'的命运：格尔茨及其他"

互动

跨学科的解释学学者都认同格尔茨对理解意义的坚持，他们尊称他为杰出的"文化理论家、民族志学者和道德哲学家"。[5]

尽管如此，格尔茨的文化概念还是在解释学学者中引起了激烈的争论。他们认为，事实证明，格尔茨关于什么是文化的传统定义已经越来越不适合现代社会。[6] 这些学者指出，当今世界包含的独特和可识别的文化越来越少，连贯的生活方式也越来越少。学者们还发现，即使是在一个家庭内，信仰、实践和情感也变得不那么统一，更不用说部落、社区、民族或文明的更大群体了。[7] 他们还认为，当今的文化是以流动的、复杂的社会形态呈现出来。现代"部落"包含全球网络、社交媒体社区和混合身份，其特征表现为全球化、复杂性和广阔性。[8] 就目前的社会和政治现象来看，格尔茨所提出的统一的、静态的、不受外界势力干扰的文化概念的有效性遭受严重质疑。

因此，学者们花了大量时间来研究文化系统概念的新思考和现代化。[9]与格尔茨一样，诸多现代民族志学者继续研究不同地区人们体验生活的不同方式。与格尔茨不同的是，他们不认为文化是封闭的和孤立的。如果说他们对格尔茨的方法进行了补充，那么，他们所做的就是通过对当地文化和文化与权力的相互作用产生影响的政治、经济、社会、历史和文化的框架进行了研究。[10]

持续争议

当代著名的文化人类学家，如雪莉·奥特纳、莉拉·阿布-卢格霍德、乔治·马库斯和罗纳托·罗萨尔多，进行了大量实践探讨以回应对格尔茨文化概念"深刻而深远"的批评。[11]辩论的主要议题包括人类学核心文化概念的重构以及全球化背景下民族志面临的现实问题。他们还对现代人类学田野调查的实践形式进行了重新审视。[12]

与格尔茨一起工作过的雪莉·奥特纳是当代一位富有影响力的文化人类学家。她对这场持续的辩论作出了有益的总结，并对富有成效的推进方案进行了思考。[13]奥特纳认为，问题不应该是摒弃还是坚持格尔茨的文化概念，进而延伸到经典的"人类学项目"。[14]她提出了一个非常有道理的观点："问题是，再一次，为不断变化的世界、不断变化的政治与学术生活之间的关系以及不断变化的理论可能性，重构这个极富成效的概念。"[15]

奥特纳提出了重新思考文化的三个必要条件。[16]首先，她建议"保持一种有关文化差异的有力假设，但要有新的研究"。[17]其次，奥特纳认为，现代思想家应该关注《文化的解释》中的意义建构问题，而不是文化系统的概念。第三，她主张学者们应该将他们的文化分析置于"对社会和政治事件及进程的更大规模的分析之下",因为"文化分析……本身不再是目的。"[18] 换言之,她呼吁学者们重视格尔茨"意义承载"和"意义建构"的观点。但她认识到,学者们必须寻求以多种新方式定位(即"发现"或"识别")和审视文化。

---

1. 波林·特纳·斯特朗:"书评论文集:人类学与跨学科的未来",《美国人类学家》第110卷,2008年6月第2期,第253页。

2. 雪莉·奥特纳:"专题:'文化'的命运:格尔茨及其他",《再现》第59卷,1997年,第1—14页。

3. 奥特纳:"专题",第6页。

4. 理查德·施韦德:"克利福德·格尔茨的果断与不决",《通识》第13卷,2007年春秋刊第2—3期,第203页。

5. 奥特纳:"专题",第2页。

6. 奥特纳:"专题",第7页。

7. 奥特纳:"专题",第7页。

8. 奥特纳:"专题",第7—8页。

9. 奥特纳:"专题",第1页。

10. 奥特纳:"专题",第7—8页。

11. 奥特纳:"专题",第8页。

12. 奥特纳:"专题",第7—9页。

13. 奥特纳:"专题",第1—14页。

14. 奥特纳:"专题",第1—14页。

15. 奥特纳:"专题",第8页。

16. 奥特纳:"专题",第8页。

17. 奥特纳:"专题",第8页。

18. 奥特纳:"专题",第9页。

12 未来展望

要点 🔑

- 《文化的解释》重视社会生活中与意义的产生和传递相关的各个方面。人们将会一直铭记这部经典著作。

- 这本开创性的论著适用于探讨"社会哲学和道德哲学问题",这种适用性似乎不会减弱。

- 在《文化的解释》中,格尔茨致力于确立什么是文化以及应该如何研究文化,引入了"深描"的概念,即对语境中的人类行为进行详细的、解释性的分析。

潜力

学者们今后仍将认同克利福德·格尔茨的《文化的解释》是一部经典之作,而格尔茨本人则被誉为"在 20 世纪下半叶,几乎凭一己之力重新划分了社会科学和人文科学的边界"。[1] 虽然自格尔茨撰写该书以来,世界发生了许多变化,但这部著作将继续为关于文化的大规模、持续辩论提供重要参考。格尔茨的核心主张具有永恒的价值和普遍的适用性。正如他的学生雪莉·奥特纳所写的那样,他想要理解"由意义的不断产生和转变所定义的人的境况。"[2] 格尔茨提出了这样一种观点,即人类存在的每一个物质、政治、社会和个人方面都是"同时被文化所定义、塑造,并承载着认知和情感意义。"在可预见的未来,学者们将会继续看到这一概念在各学科之间的连锁反应。[3]

然而,仍有一些学者指出了这部著作中的不足之处。他们指出，《文化的解释》忽略了权力、冲突和不平等的问题。[4]批评家们认为，这本书在政治上并不进步，在道德上过于中立，对某种文化概念过于关注，在应该解释的地方过于偏重描述。[5]尽管如此，学者们断言，《文化的解释》无论对是作为一门科学的人类学政治还是人类学领域范围内的政治都具有重要意义。这些在未来仍将适用。[6]在解决"社会哲学和道德哲学问题"方面，这部著作的理论实用性也依然不会减弱。[7]

正因如此，奥特纳提出，在我们强调社会生活的"意义承载"和"意义建构"方面（社会生活中那些与意义的传递或意义的产生有关的部分）时，我们会继续设想一种"本质上是格尔茨式的观点"。[8]

> "文化，如果继续将其理解为社会进程的一个重要组成部分，那么，就必须以非常不同的方式来对其进行定位和审视，将其看作：边界地区的意义冲突；具有自身连贯性，但始终在本地受到解释的公共文化；在噩梦般的情况下由弱势行为者编织的脆弱的故事网和意义网；不断发展的社会实践中的代理性和意向性的基础。"
> —— 雪莉·奥特纳："专题：'文化'的命运：格尔茨及其他"

未来方向

这部著作在未来几乎肯定会用于人类学的自我质疑。我们很可能看到诸多进一步更新格尔茨的文化概念的研究尝试。学者们也可能试图重新定义他对人类学的理解，将其与格尔茨撰写这部著作以来出现的多维度的社会形态联系起来。这些复杂的社会形态包括民族、跨国网络、不断变化的话语（当我们思考或谈论某些主题时所运用的语言系统和假设系统）、全球"流动"（商品、人员、思想、技术等的流动）、越来越混杂的身份、社交媒介团体等等。

奥特纳总结了指导未来学者的首要问题："在存在着这些形态和进程的世界中，人类学如何才能在最深层意义上对民族志作品进行长期的、认真的、文采斐然的、全身心的、参与性的观察？在民族志作品的牢固地域性、实地考察性和这些形态的广泛性、复杂性，尤其是非地域性之间，可以 / 可能 / 应该获得什么样的关系？"[9]

最近，一些文化学者认为他们的研究并不符合格尔茨的观点。事实上，他们并不认为自己与文化人类学有关。但是现代文化人类学家如雪莉·奥特纳、罗纳托·罗萨尔多、莉拉·阿布-卢格霍德指出了一个方向，即欢迎"文化间摩擦区域的民族志和历史，其中权力、意义和身份的冲突处于变化和转变之中"。[10] 例如，奥特纳写了一本书，探讨喜马拉雅山登山运动中的冲突历史。[11] 一方面，她论述了西方登山运动员，这些人在她看来相当"野蛮"，其中一个原因是，他们坚持在探险过程中屠宰动物作为肉食；另一方面，她发现珠穆朗玛峰周围地区的居民是信奉佛教的夏尔巴人*——尽管他们自己并不完全是非暴力的，但对杀生深恶痛绝。

小结

在《文化的解释》中，克利福德·格尔茨进行了界定"什么是文化，文化在社会生活中扮演什么角色，以及应该如何对其进行适当的研究"的学术挑战。[12] 格尔茨研究文化的独特方法集中在解开同一群体的人们主观上所共有的意义之网。格尔茨研究了文化中的象征，并发现它们包含着各种意义体系。[13]

最重要的是，这部开创性的著作促成了 20 世纪美国现代文化人类学的新兴趋势。格尔茨帮助他的同行关注人们如何看待自己和自己生活的世界。他特别注意工艺品和神话等象征。《文化的解释》提出了著名的"深描"概念，格尔茨运用这个解释性的过程解释了特定象征行为对其行为的个人主体所具有的共同意义。深描有助于他尝试阐述"由此获得的知识对它所处的社会以及更广泛的社会生活能够揭示什么"。[14] 对许多该领域之内或之外的人而言，深描不仅解释了格尔茨的工作，而且也解释了文化人类学家的总体研究。[15] 深描集中于意义的构建——即行动获得象征意义的方式——和解释。这使得文化人类学比自然科学 * 更接近人文学科。格尔茨与马歇尔·萨林斯、大卫·施耐德、维克多·特纳和玛丽·道格拉斯等人一起，成为20世纪60年代"象征性"或"解释性"思想学派的主要代表人物。

1. 雪莉·奥特纳："专题：'文化'的命运：格尔茨及其他"，《再现》第 59 卷，1997 年，第 1 页。
2. 奥特纳："克利福德·格尔茨（1926—2006）"，《美国人类学家》第 109 卷，2007 年第 4 期，第 786 页。
3. 奥特纳："克利福德·格尔茨（1926—2006）"，第 787 页。
4. 爱德华·布鲁纳："《克利福德·格尔茨：他的批评者与追随者》书评，1998 年"，《人类学与人文主义》第 23 卷，1998 年第 2 期，第 216 页。
5. 阿兰姆·延戈扬："克利福德·格尔茨、文化肖像与东南亚"，《亚洲研究期刊》第 68 卷，2009 年 11 月第 4 期，第 1217 页。
6. 奥特纳："专题"，第 4 页。
7. 奥特纳："专题"，第 5 页。
8. 奥特纳："专题"，第 11 页。

9. 奥特纳："专题"，第7—8页。

10. 奥特纳："专题"，第8页。

11. 雪莉·奥特纳：《珠穆朗玛峰上的生与死：夏尔巴人与喜马拉雅登山运动》，普林斯顿：普林斯顿大学出版社，1999年。

12. 克利福德·格尔茨：《文化的解释》，第2版，纽约：基础书局，2000年，第vii页。

13. 格尔茨：《文化的解释》，第125页。

14. 格尔茨：《文化的解释》，第26—27页。

15. 奥特纳："克利福德·格尔茨（1926—2006）"，第787页。

术语表

1. **反犹太主义**：对犹太人的歧视、偏见或敌意。

2. **考古人类学**：有关远古人类文化的起源、成长和发展的研究。

3. **生物人类学**：有关人类物种进化的研究。

4. **佛教夏尔巴人**：居住在珠穆朗玛峰周边地区并遵从藏传佛教传统的人。

5. **认知人类学**：人类学的一个分支，研究人类的认知是如何影响他们感知周围环境及理解这个世界的。

6. **冷战**：从 1947 年到 1991 年，美国及其西方盟国和苏联之间的紧张时期。

7. **殖民主义**：强行夺取对另一个国家的控制权，使非本国居民定居该国，并侵占其资源和资产的行为。

8. **语境的**：基于具体的情况和情境。

9. **文化人类学**：人类学的一个分支，研究人类文化的根源、历史和发展。

10. **文化**：根据格尔茨的观点，文化是一种共享意义系统，应该通过解释该文化的象征（如艺术和神话）来研究。

11. **网络欺凌**：西方社会年轻人普遍存在的一种行为，即通过使用电脑和手机进行在线互动，来孤立和欺负同龄人。

12. **生态人类学**：研究人类与其生物物理环境之间关系的学科。

13. **天国的**：属于或关于天堂的。

14. **民族志**：研究文化现象并以实地研究或个案研究的书面方式记录其发现的研究。

15. **功能主义**：一种通过分析社会元素如何运作来分析社会的观点。

16. **全球变暖**：地球大气温度上升，可能造成非常严重的影响，部分原因是人类活动导致大气中温室气体的增加。

17. **历史特殊主义**：一种观点，认为每个社会都是其特定历史进程的产物。

18. **整体主义**：认为事物的各个部分是紧密相连的，只有参照整体才能加以解释。

19. **艾克拉斯**：爪哇人对死亡的超然接受的概念。

20. **印度尼西亚**：印度尼西亚共和国，由东南亚数千个岛屿组成的群岛。

21. **跨学科**：利用几个不同学科的目标和方法进行的研究。

22. **解释方法或解释主义**：在人类学中，这种方法认为人类学家应该理解人们和文化是如何看待他们自己的，然后再将这种文化意义翻译给外界。

23. **语言人类学**：研究代表文化的语言的学科。

24. **马克思主义**：德国政治哲学家卡尔·马克思在 19 世纪提出的一种社会经济和政治世界观。这些观点是基于他对于资本主义是如何发展和影响阶级斗争的主张而发展起来的。

25. **唯物主义**：认为除了物质之外什么都不存在，因此事物只能通过感官来衡量或认识。

26. **自然科学**：描述、预测和理解自然现象并揭示"自然规律"的科学分支。

27. **参与性观察**：一种数据收集方法，研究人员通过融入、观察和参与研究对象的社交生活来获取数据。

28. **特殊主义**：仅服务于个人利益、团体、政党或国家。

29. **实证主义**：一种拒绝内省和直觉知识的观点。实证主义者认为，只有逻辑和数学方法在揭示社会规律方面是科学的和值得信赖的。

30. **后殖民主义**：20世纪中叶，前殖民国家独立后出现的一种学术方向（有时也指"时代"或"理论"）。作为一种学术方法，后殖民主义研究分析殖民时期的各种文化、语言和社会遗产。

31. **相对主义**：这种概念认为，观点没有绝对的真理或有效性，只能根据不同的人对它们的感知和思考，留取其相对的、主观的价值。

32. **再现**：一种表演或演绎，尤其是对戏剧角色或音乐作品的表演。

33. **鲁昆**：爪哇人的社会和谐观。

34. **符号学**：对符号和符号系统的研究，包括语言的和非语言的符号以及它们的传播方式。

35. **社会人类学**：研究社会结构及其在人类文化中的作用。

36. **社会革命**：由人民（而不是政党）发起的革命，以重组社会为目的，如1954至1968年的美国民权运动。

37. **社会学**：研究社会行为、社会制度以及人类社会的起源和组织的学科。

38. **结构主义**：一种认为应从更大的、总体的系统或结构的关系来理解人类文化元素的理论。

39. **主观性**：一个人的观点是受他或她个人的独特感知、经历、信仰和欲望所影响的。

40. **象征人类学**：人类学的一个分支，将文化视为一套象征系统，并通过研究仪式和符号来揭示其文化意义。

41. **深描**：该描述方式不仅解释特定的人类行为，而且还解释了这种行为的具体语境，以使文化外的人充分理解其意义。

42. **深入理解（维斯特恩）**：德语单词 Verstehen，意为对人类行为的深刻理解。

43. **虚拟朋友**：通过社交网络服务、留言板、共享兴趣网站等在线交互而认识的人。

44. **第二次世界大战**（1935—1945）：轴心国（德国、意大利和日本）与同盟国（英国及其殖民地、苏联和美国）之间的全球范围的冲突，同盟国一方最终获胜。

人名表

1. **莉拉·阿布–卢格霍德**（1952 年生），拥有巴勒斯坦和犹太血统的美国人类学家。她的研究兴趣集中在民族主义、媒介、性别政治和记忆政治上。她写了一篇被广为转载的文章"穆斯林妇女真的需要拯救吗？"（2002）。

2. **塔拉尔·阿萨德**（1932 年生），人类学家，以在后殖民主义、基督教、伊斯兰教和仪式研究方面的著作而闻名。

3. **简·奥斯汀**（1775—1817），英国小说家。代表作有《理智与情感》（1811）、《傲慢与偏见》（1813）和《爱玛》（1815）。

4. **凯伦·布鲁**（1941 年生），纽约大学的人类学荣誉教授，因对美洲印第安人的研究而闻名。

5. **弗朗茨·博厄斯**（1858—1942），现代美国人类学的创始人。他建立了文化相对论的概念，并认为全人类智力相当。1920 年，他撰写了纲领性文章《民族学方法论》。

6. **皮埃尔·布尔迪厄**（1930—2002），法国社会学家、哲学家和人类学家。布尔迪厄一生出版著作约 30 余部，撰写题材广泛的论文 300 多篇。他的文风具有经验主义色彩和较强的理论性，使一些读者望而却步。

7. **玛丽·道格拉斯**（1921—2007），英国人类学家。她的群体／格栅文化研究图式为文化理论奠定了基础，她有关风险分析的著作开创了经济人类学。其最负盛名的著作为《纯净与危险：对污染与禁忌等观念的分析》，首次发表于 1966 年。

8. **路易·杜蒙**（1911—1998），专门致力于研究印度的法国人类学家。他因在印度种姓和血缘关系方面所做的工作在人类学家中享有盛名。

9. **埃米尔·杜尔凯姆**（1858—1917），法国社会学家、心理学家和哲学家。杜尔凯姆与政治哲学家卡尔·马克思和社会学家马克斯·韦伯以建立现代社会学而闻名。他最负盛名的代表作《自杀论》（1897）探讨了不同人群中的自杀行为。

10. 查尔斯·弗雷克（1930年生），20世纪语言人类学家。1969年，发表了《认知系统的民族志研究》。

11. 西格蒙德·弗洛伊德（1856—1939），奥地利神经学家，现在被誉为现代精神分析的创始人。

12. 希尔德雷德·斯托里·格尔茨（1929年生），普林斯顿大学人类学荣誉教授，曾讲授有关人类学理论史、艺术人类学和民族志艺术的课程。在爪哇、摩洛哥和巴厘岛进行实地研究。

13. 乔治·R.盖格（1903—1998），美国安提阿学院的哲学教授。他于1937年由著名哲学家约翰·杜威推荐加入了该学院，1969年正式退休后继续在该校任教。他成为亨利·乔治哲学的最著名的"解释者"之一。

14. 马文·哈里斯（1927—2001），一位在文化唯物主义发展中有影响力的美国人类学家。他的《人类学理论的兴起：文化理论史》是人类学界的权威著作。

15. 罗杰·基辛（1935—1993），人类学家，他以研究所罗门群岛马莱塔岛的槐欧族人而闻名。他的研究涉及亲属关系、宗教、政治和语言。

16. 克莱德·克拉克洪（1905—1960），哈佛大学社会人类学和社会关系学教授。以研究纳瓦霍人的语言和文化，发展了一种称为"价值取向理论"的方法论而著称。

17. 克劳德·列维-斯特劳斯（1908—2009），法国社会人类学家，致力于建立和倡导结构主义方面的研究，该研究分析诸如亲属关系等文化系统的结构。

18. 乔治·马库斯（1968年生），美国文化人类学家，致力于研究权力及其对普通人的影响。马库斯于1986年创办了期刊《文化人类学》。

19. 布罗尼斯拉夫·马林诺夫斯基（1884—1942），20 世纪最有影响力的人类学家之一。他以建立社会人类学而闻名，他的大多数研究是关于大洋洲民族的。

20. 卡尔·马克思（1818—1883），哲学家、社会学家和经济学家。他的著作为 20 世纪很多共产主义政权奠定了基础，也因此为他赢得了共产主义革命者的盛名。其代表作《资本论》于 1867 年到 1894 年间分三卷出版。

21. C. 赖特·米尔斯（1916—1962），美国社会学家，从 1946 年开始在哥伦比亚大学工作直至去世。他最著名的代表作包括《白领》（1951）、《权力精英》（1956）和《社会学的想象力》（1959）。

22. 雪莉·奥特纳（1941 年生），文化人类学家，曾师从克利福德·格尔茨，并以其关于转型和抵抗的理论而闻名。

23. 塔尔科特·帕森斯（1902—1979），被广泛认为是 20 世纪最具影响力的美国社会学家之一。他将社会学先驱马克斯·韦伯引入美国学术界，并且还主张关注人们的主观现实。他的主要著作包括《社会行动的结构》（1937）和《社会系统》（1951）。

24. 阿尔弗雷德·拉德克利夫-布朗（1881—1955），英国社会人类学家。他的研究主要关注前工业社会的社会结构的运作方式，他在此基础上发展了他的功能主义理论。

25. 罗伊·拉帕波特（1926—1997），人类学家，主要致力于仪式和生态人类学方面的研究。

26. 理查德·罗蒂（1931—2007），颇具影响力的、务实的美国哲学家。他的主要著作包括《哲学和自然之镜》（1979）。

27. 罗纳托·罗萨尔多（1941 年生），世界领先的文化人类学家之一，研究方向为文化公民身份。

28. 吉尔伯特·赖尔（1900—1976），英国哲学家，主要研究语言的本质和用法。以其主张心灵的运作与身体的行为有关而闻名，代表作为《心的概念》（1949）。

29. **马歇尔·萨林斯**（1930年生），芝加哥大学的人类学家。他的研究领域侧重于文化在塑造人们的观念和行为方面的作用。

30. **费尔迪南·德·索绪尔**（1857—1913），瑞士语言学家，被认为是现代语言学和意义建构（即意义指称）研究的创始人。他的代表作是在他过世后出版的语言学讲稿。

31. **大卫·M.施奈德**（1918—1995），象征人类学方法的主要倡导者，尤以他对亲属关系的研究而闻名。

32. **理查德·施韦德**（1945年生），美国文化人类学家，他的著作有《通过文化思考：文化心理学探险》（1991）和《为什么男人要烧烤？文化心理学食谱》（2003）。

33. **詹姆斯·斯普拉德利**（1933—1982），著作甚丰的美国人类学家，他认为研究人员应该寻找研究对象对他们的生活所赋予的意义。

34. **维克托·特纳**（1920—1983），苏格兰人类学家，以其对仪式和成年礼的研究而闻名。

35. **爱德华·伯内特·泰勒**（1832—1917），英国人类学家，被认为是文化人类学的创立者。其最具影响力的作品为《原始文化》（1871）。

36. **安德鲁·P.瓦伊达**（1931年生），生态人类学家，专门研究方法论和解释。他主要探讨了印度尼西亚和巴布亚新几内亚社会科学与生态科学之间的关系。

37. **马克斯·韦伯**（1864—1920），德国社会学家。与法国社会理论家埃米尔·杜尔凯姆、德国政治哲学家卡尔·马克思一起，被学术界誉为社会学的奠基人。他以其对官僚主义的见解和极具影响力的论文《新教伦理与资本主义精神》（1934）而闻名。

38. **阿兰姆·延戈扬**（1936年生），美国人类学教授，对东南亚有独到的研究。

WAYS IN TO THE TEXT

- The American cultural anthropologist* Clifford Geertz conducted extensive field research in the Pacific nation of Indonesia,* which inspired the essays in his 1973 publication *The Interpretation of Cultures.* Geertz died in 2006.

- Cultural anthropology looks at the variations among human cultures. Many considered Geertz the most important cultural anthropologist in the United States.

- Geertz defined culture* as a system of shared meaning that ought to be studied by interpreting the symbols of that culture, such as art and myths. *The Interpretation of Cultures* came to define the field. Although the general public often misunderstood the book, it remains one of the most cited works among academics across disciplines.

Who Was Clifford Geertz?

The cultural anthropologist Clifford Geertz is best known for his 1973 work *The Interpretation of Cultures.* He was born on August 23, 1926 in San Francisco in the United States. Geertz was only three years old when his father and mother split up. He was then taken in by foster parents who lived in a rural part of California. At the age of 17, Geertz signed up with the US Navy. Following two years of military service, Geertz left the Navy at the end of World War II* in 1945.

After the war, Geertz went to study at Antioch College in Ohio with funding from the GI Bill (money granted by the government to veterans of World War II), and graduated in 1950 with a degree in philosophy. He moved on to graduate school at the prestigious Harvard University, studying with two famous scholars: Clyde Kluckhohn,* a professor of anthropology, and Talcott Parsons,* a professor of sociology.* Geertz obtained his doctorate in anthropology in 1956.

In the 15 years that followed, Geertz produced the essays eventually collected in *The Interpretation of Cultures*. These essays evolved from insights he gained from field research in Bali, Java, and Sumatra, three islands in the Indonesian archipelago. He conducted his research there with his first wife, Hildred Storey Geertz,* also a famous anthropologist.

In 1970 Geertz became a professor of social science at the Institute for Advanced Study in Princeton, New Jersey, where he worked for 30 years until the end of his career. Clifford and Hildred had no children and divorced after 32 years. Geertz later married Karen Blu,* another anthropologist, and they had two children together.

Geertz never recovered from heart surgery and died on October 30, 2006. The cultural anthropologist Richard Allan Shweder,* who studied with Geertz, described him as "an unpretentious, even somewhat introverted man, who was skittish and halting yet also riveting and dazzling in interpersonal encounters."[1]

What Does *The Interpretation of Cultures* Say?

The Interpretation of Cultures, published in 1973, set out "a treatise in cultural theory."[2] The book formally and systematically explains what culture is and how we ought to study it. It helped redefine the discipline of anthropology. It also influenced the emergence of cultural anthropology, which studies the cultural variations between different peoples and societies, as well as how people behave, communicate, and socialize with one another.

Geertz defined culture as "a system of inherited conceptions expressed in symbolic forms."[3] In other words, he viewed culture as an organized collection of symbols and signs that carry particular meaning. For example, the statue of the dying Jesus on a cross is a symbol that carries a religious meaning and forms part of a cultural system called religion. Even people who are not religious and therefore outsiders to this particular cultural system recognize the symbol.

Based on his concept of culture, Geertz believed we ought to study it in a particular way. In *The Interpretation of Cultures*, he offered two key ideas about how to do that.

First, he suggested that anthropologists can only understand culture properly if they look at how people express themselves through symbols, signs, symbolic acts, and rituals. For example, for Christians, eating bread and drinking wine during a Church service is a symbolic act. It represents eating the flesh and drinking the blood of Christ. The members of this culture, then, use these symbolic acts to celebrate the love of their God that transforms death into new life.

Second, Geertz says anthropologists ought to study culture from the perspective of the people concerned. He believes that "cultures and peoples should speak for themselves, with anthropologists learning to converse with them and interpret them."[4] In other words, culture ought to be interpreted from the viewpoint of the person whose culture it actually is.

This means that anthropologists should read the meanings of symbols or symbolic acts just as native people do, and then translate and convey their meanings to outsiders. Geertz calls this process an interpretive approach.* Interpretive scholars must explain and clarify the realities that different groups of people have built in their social world.

Of course, all interpretations must necessarily be rooted in a particular moment. They apply to a specific time, context, and situation. Having said that, conversations can cause interpretations to be revised and renegotiated to a certain extent. Because of this, the interpretivist approach Geertz lays out suggests researchers can only produce adequate interpretations if they view the world through the eyes of the people they seek to understand.

Why Does *The Interpretation of Cultures* Matter?

The Interpretation of Cultures established Geertz as "a major voice" of the "symbolic" or interpretive anthropology movement of the 1960s.[5] For many people, both inside and outside of the discipline, *The Interpretation of Cultures* explained not only what Geertz did, but also what cultural anthropologists in general do.[6]

The Interpretation of Cultures also influenced how cultural anthropology is done today. Geertz said that nurturing a dialogue between researcher and subject is crucial. Doing this requires carefully observing and interviewing people about the meanings of their symbols and symbolic actions. Working this way gives

81

anthropologists a more informed and sophisticated understanding of what they examine. It also enables them to see better how people understand themselves, others, and the world around them. Such an understanding in turn helps anthropologists develop more comprehensive and representative interpretations of societies.

The Interpretation of Cultures shows us a way to understand different ways of life.[7] Given the world's ever increasing cultural, moral, scientific, and political diversity, understanding our differences remains as relevant and timely today as it was when Geertz was working in the 1960s. As the influential cultural anthropologist Sherry Ortner* argues, Geertz's book has a "timeless quality" and is useful for everyone.[8]

The Interpretation of Cultures was among the most cited works in the 2007 *Handbook of Cultural Psychology*.[9] The *New York Times Literary Supplement* called it "one of the 100 most important books since World War II."[10] It remains essential reading for anyone who wants to interpret the meanings of people's actions in the world.[11]

---

1. Richard Shweder, *Clifford James Geertz: 1926–2006, A Biographical Memoir* (Washington, DC: National Academy of Sciences), 5, accessed November 2, 2015, https://www.sss.ias.edu/files/pdfs/Geertz_NAS_6-10-10.pdf.
2. Clifford Geertz, *The Interpretation of Cultures*, 2nd edn (New York: Basic Books, 2000), viii.
3. Geertz, *The Interpretation of Cultures*, 89.
4. Andrew Yarrow, "Clifford Geertz, Cultural Anthropologist, Is Dead at 80," *New York Times*, November 1, 2006, accessed December 8, 2015, http://www.nytimes.com/2006/11/01/obituaries/01geertz. html?pagewanted=print&_r=0.

5. Richard Shweder, "The Resolute Irresolution of Clifford Geertz," *Common Knowledge* 13, nos. 2–3 (Spring-Fall 2007): 191–205.

6. Richard Shweder and Byron Good, eds., *Clifford Geertz by His Colleagues* (Chicago: University of Chicago Press, 2005).

7. Shweder, "The Resolute Irresolution of Clifford Geertz," 203.

8. Sherry Ortner, "Special Issue: The Fate of 'Culture': Geertz and beyond," *Representations* 59 (1997): 7.

9. Shweder, "The Resolute Irresolution of Clifford Geertz," 203.

10. Yarrow, "Clifford Geertz."

11. See Ortner, "Special Issue," 7.

SECTION 1
INFLUENCES

THE AUTHOR AND THE HISTORICAL CONTEXT

KEY POINTS

* Scholars consider *The Interpretation of Cultures* one of the founding texts of interpretive anthropology* (an approach to anthropological research that proposes that peoples and cultures should represent themselves, and that anthropologists should learn to interpret cultural meanings to outsiders).

* A range of academic disciplines influenced Geertz's work, evidenced by his lifelong passion for interdisciplinary* experimentation; "interdisciplinary" refers to research that draws on the aims and methods of different academic disciplines.

* By the 1960s, the field of anthropology sought to distance itself from its colonial* origins (its origins in the period of European political and economic exploitation of foreign territories and people, particularly in the nineteenth century) and reinvent itself as an area of study that explores the ways people see themselves and their world.

Why Read This Text?

Arguing for the need to embrace an interpretive approach to the field of anthropology, Clifford Geertz's *The Interpretation of Cultures* (1973) remains essential reading for students of this discipline.

In it, Geertz proposes that interpretive anthropology has two purposes: first, to see the world through the eyes of those born into a given culture; second, to translate the resulting insight to those outside the culture—an approach known as interpretivism.

The interpretive approach to studying culture revolutionized the field of anthropology. Geertz was among the first generation of scholars to propose that outsiders should study culture by understanding the subjective perspectives of those living in the culture (that is, the world as it was understood by people from other cultures). Until then, practitioners had believed that anthropologists should study a culture "objectively from the outside" as detached observers.[1] Aram Yengoyan,* a well-respected social anthropologist* (a scholar of social structures and their role in human cultures) with particular expertise in southeast Asia, has argued that *The Interpretation of Cultures* offered a new form of anthropology. Geertz's approach differed significantly from the anthropology advocated by his contemporaries.[2]

The Interpretation of Cultures also made an impact beyond the confines of anthropology, influencing disciplines in the social sciences and humanities. The academic world recognized the importance of *The Interpretation of Cultures* immediately following its publication in 1973. Only a year later, the volume won the 1974 Sorokin Award of the American Sociological Association. When the work was republished in 2000, *The New York Times* celebrated it as "one of the 100 most important books since World War II."*[3] But the general public never fully appreciated the importance of Geertz's book.

> *"Let me instead take the rather peculiar tack of thanking three remarkable academic institutions that have provided me with the kind of setting for scholarly work I am convinced could not be surpassed right now anywhere in the world: The Department of Social Relations of Harvard University, where I was trained; the Department of Anthropology of the University of Chicago, where I taught for a decade; and The Institute for Advanced Study in Princeton, where I now work."*
>
> —— Clifford Geertz, *The Interpretation of Cultures*

Author's Life

Clifford Geertz was born in 1926 in San Francisco, a city in the US state of California. His parents separated when Geertz was three years old, and sent him to rural California to be brought up by foster parents. When Geertz turned 17, he enlisted with the US Navy. He served in World War II from 1943 until 1945.

Following his naval service, Geertz studied philosophy at Antioch College in Ohio, where the philosopher George Geiger* mentored him. After graduating in 1950, Geertz applied for a PhD at Harvard University's newly founded interdisciplinary Department of Social Relations.[4] Two famous American scholars led this department: the sociologist* Talcott Parsons* and the cultural anthropologist* Clyde Kluckhohn;* sociology is the study of the nature and history of human society, while cultural anthropology is the study of human beliefs and practices as they are understood to constitute "culture." Geertz later reported that the unique academic culture of the new department at Harvard infected him with "a great excitement about interdisciplinary experimentation."[5] This would become a lifelong characteristic and integral part of his work.

In 1960, Geertz joined the Anthropology Department at the distinguished University of Chicago. During his decade in Chicago, Geertz championed his particular concept of culture.[6] In 1970, he moved to Princeton University, becoming a professor of social science at the Institute for Advanced Study. He stayed there for the rest of his career, becoming a professor emeritus in 2000. In Princeton, Geertz established himself as what Peter Goddard, director of the institute, described as a "major intellectual figure of the twentieth century."[7] His most influential works include *The Religion of Java* (1960); *Person, Time, and Conduct in Bali* (1966); *The Interpretation of Cultures* (1973); *Local Knowledge: Further Essays in Interpretive Anthropology* (1983); and *Works and Lives: The Anthropologist as Author* (1988).[8]

Author's Background

Clifford Geertz wrote *The Interpretation of Cultures* in the 1960s, a period of upheaval in society and politics. In particular, these years were marked by postcolonialism* (a theoretical current relating to the various social, philosophical, and linguistic legacies of the colonial period) and social revolutions* (active, popular expressions of discontent with existing social systems). In the wake of these revolutions, "anthropology was torn apart by questions about its colonial past."[9]

To understand this past, we need to look back to the

seventeenth and the eighteenth centuries. Anthropologists in the colonial era were dedicated to "scientifically" researching the cultures of the colonies. But they approached their inquiries with a bias that read Europeans and European society as biologically and culturally superior to all others, seeing colonized people as undeveloped and in need of being "civilized." This facilitated the rise in imperialism in Western Europe through the nineteenth and early twentieth centuries, as regimes used these theories to justify the expansion of their colonial empires.

In the early twentieth century, colonial administrations tasked anthropologists with studying the colonized, including addressing specific questions such as how the colonized people responded to colonial policies, such as the imposition of certain taxes.[10] Again, this was "science" in the service of a particular end, not objective inquiry.

Many colonial territories achieved independence after the Declaration on the Granting of Independence to Colonial Countries and Peoples, adopted by the United Nations in 1960. People began to question the involvement of anthropologists in colonialism and the relevance and ethics of the field in general.[11] This was the background against which Geertz conducted his anthropological work.

1. Institute for Advanced Study, "Clifford Geertz 1926–2006," accessed December 8, 2015, https://www.ias.edu/news/press-releases/2009–49.

2. Aram Yengoyan, "Clifford Geertz, Cultural Portraits, and Southeast Asia," *The Journal of Asian Studies* 68, no. 4 (November 2009): 1215–17.

3. Andrew Yarrow, "Clifford Geertz, Cultural Anthropologist, Is Dead at 80," *New York Times*, November 1, 2006, accessed December 8, 2015, http://www.nytimes.com/2006/11/01/obituaries/01geertz. html?pagewanted=print&_r=0.

4. Institute for Advanced Study, "Geertz."

5. Clifford Geertz, "Passage and Accident: A Life of Learning," in *Available Light: Anthropological Reflections on Philosophical Topics*, by Clifford Geertz (Princeton: Princeton University Press, 2000), 7.

6. Clifford Geertz, *The Interpretation of Cultures*, 2nd edn (New York: Basic Books, 2000), 89.

7. Institute for Advanced Study, "Geertz."

8. See Clifford Geertz, *The Religion of Java* (Glencoe: The Free Press, *1960*); *Person, Time, and Conduct in Bali: An Essay in Cultural Analysis* (New Haven: Yale University Southeast Asia Studies, 1966); *Local Knowledge: Further Essays in Interpretive Anthropology* (New York: Basic Books, 1983); *Works and Lives: The Anthropologist as Author* (Stanford: Stanford University Press, 1988).

9. Institute for Advanced Study, "Geertz."

10. For a critical history of colonial anthropology, see Diane Lewis, "Anthropology and Colonialism," *Current Anthropology* 14, no. 5 (December 1973): 581–602.

11. Lewis, "Anthropology and Colonialism," 581.

MODULE 2
ACADEMIC CONTEXT

KEY POINTS

* Anthropology concerns itself with the study of human cultures.

* In 1871 the English anthropologist Sir Edward Burnett Tylor* laid the foundations of cultural anthropology* with his famous book *Primitive Culture*.[1]

* Like his academic predecessors, Geertz believed in the continued importance of anthropology as an academic discipline. Unlike prior academics, he believed that anthropologists must interpret other cultures not from the outside, but from the cultures' own point of view.

The Work in Its Context

When Clifford Geertz wrote *The Interpretation of Cultures* (1973), a new generation of scholars was emerging, holding the belief that anthropologists ought to study a culture from the perspectives of the people living in that culture. Colonial anthropologists had studied cultures "objectively from the outside." They believed that only European colonizers had the scientific capacity to discern a people's culture.[2] Geertz wrote his book at a time when anthropologists were beginning to challenge these colonial practices and perspectives.

To achieve "insider" understanding, anthropologists of the new generation lived in the midst of the subjects of their studies. Scholars call this participant observation.* These participant-anthropologists carefully recorded every small detail regarding the culture of the people and their communal lives, and attempted to explain their meanings. Scholars call this process and the reports that result ethnography.*To this day, anthropologists continue to explore cultural phenomena using ethnography.

In *The Interpretation of Cultures*, Geertz put forward a particular approach to doing ethnography. He based it on his conceptualization of culture as a collection of symbols and symbolic rites that have specific meaning. Geertz's particular approach to understanding and researching culture helped anthropology distance itself from its colonial heritage and reinvent itself as a discipline.

The Interpretation of Cultures also helped to define a specific branch of anthropology—cultural anthropology. This usually refers to ethnographic works that are holistic* in spirit (aiming, that is, to provide a rounded, integrated view of a people's knowledge, customs, and practices). *The Interpretation of Cultures* contributed to an emerging trend of modern cultural anthropology in the twentieth-century United States. In the 1960s it became known as the symbolic or interpretive anthropology movement.

> "[The essays that comprise The Interpretation of Cultures] all argue, sometimes explicitly, more often merely through the particular analysis they develop, for a narrowed, specialized, and, so I imagine, theoretically more powerful concept of culture to replace E. B. Tylor's famous 'most complex whole', which, its originative power not denied, seems to me to have reached the point where it obscures a good deal more than it reveals."
>
> ——Clifford Geertz, *The Interpretation of Cultures*

Overview of the Field

Until *The Interpretation of Cultures*, anthropologists had rooted their definition of culture in the British anthropologist Edward Burnett Tylor's concept of the term. In 1871, Tylor defined culture as "that complex whole that includes knowledge, belief, art, morals, law, custom and any other capabilities and habits acquired by man as a member of a society."[3] This explanation is the backbone of anthropology's modern concept of culture.

In the 1920s and 1930s, the German-born American anthropologist Franz Boas* significantly shaped the discipline in the United States. Boas believed that anthropologists should conduct in-depth research on specific cultures. He was convinced that each society exists as a collective representation of its unique historical past. This theoretical approach was called "historical particularism."*

In the meantime, Bronisław Malinowski* of Poland and Alfred Radcliffe-Brown* of England had become major figures in modern European anthropology. Their way of researching culture involved analyzing how cultural conventions ensure that a society functions. For that reason, their theoretical approach was called functionalism.* A functionalist study, for instance, would examine initiation ceremonies for adolescents. According to functionalism, initiation ceremonies served as a rite of passage into adulthood, and so their unique characteristics took on that function within a particular society.

In the 1950s, an influential anthropologist from France, Claude Lévi-Strauss,* advocated a theoretical and methodological approach called structuralism.* Structuralism focused on the contrasting relationship between the elements of a system. For example, Lévi-Strauss suggested that most prevalent cultural patterns—such as those apparent in language, ritual, and myth—could be ordered in sets of opposing concepts, such as black and white, male and female, or day and night.

Geertz rejected Boas's theory of culture. He found it too broad—covering too many areas—and too universal, because it was rooted in Tylor's definition of culture as applying to all people, everywhere. Geertz referred to it as "a conceptual morass."[4] He also never completely accepted the European anthropologists' proposition that cultural practices serve particular functions. Geertz agreed with Lévi-Strauss on the importance of symbols and symbolic action, but he disagreed with his method for examining them. In contrast to Lévi-Strauss, Geertz believed that symbols—but not their contrasting relationships—could explain social context. Geertz argued that symbols derive their meanings not from their relationships with each other, but from the roles they play in people's lives.

Academic Influences

Geertz studied for his PhD at Harvard University in Cambridge, Massachusetts, which had just established an interdisciplinary* Department of Social Relations. His studies there shaped Geertz's intellectual development significantly. Its influence can clearly be seen in his essays in *The Interpretation of Cultures*. Geertz recognized early that insights gained in a variety of disciplines in the social sciences, arts, and humanities—such as language, philosophy, sociology,* history, and literature—could help explain and analyze phenomena in anthropology. So he drew on all these disciplines to examine the meanings embodied in symbols.[5]

At Harvard, Geertz studied with the anthropologist Clyde Kluckhohn,* who introduced him to cultural anthropology. Kluckhohn also contributed to Geertz's lifelong preoccupation with symbols and symbolic action and their role in embodying patterns of meaning. The sociologist Talcott Parsons* also played a significant role in Geertz's development at Harvard. Parsons introduced Geertz to the work of Max Weber,* a German sociologist. Gilbert Ryle,* an English philosopher of language, also influenced Geertz. Ryle concluded that the way the mind works is not different from the actions of the body. In other words, the mental vocabulary is simply another way to describe action. Scholars consider Weber one of the three founding architects of sociology, together with the French thinker Émile Durkheim* and the German political philosopher Karl Marx.* Weber's social theory informed Geertz's interpretive approach to meaning. Geertz particularly adopted the Weberian belief that scholars cannot interpret people's actions unless they understand the meanings individuals attach to those actions.

---

1. See Edward Burnett Tylor, *Primitive Culture: Researches into the Development of Mythology, Philosophy, Religion, Language, Art and Custom,* 2 vols. (London: John Murray, 1871).

2. Institute for Advanced Study, "Clifford Geertz 1926–2006," accessed December 8, 2015, https://www.ias.edu/news/press-releases/2009-49.

3. Joan Leopold, *Culture in Comparative and Evolutionary Perspective: E. B. Tylor and the Making of Primitive Culture* (Berlin: Dietrich Reimer Verlag, 1980).

4. Clifford Geertz, *The Interpretation of Cultures*, 2nd edn (New York: Basic Books, 2000), 4.

5. Clifford Geertz, "Passage and Accident: A Life of Learning," in *Available Light: Anthropological Reflections on Philosophical Topics*, by Clifford Geertz (Princeton: Princeton University Press, 2000), 7.

THE PROBLEM

KEY POINTS

* Geertz's book redefines culture and the task of anthropologists.
* At the time when Geertz was writing, most anthropologists argued that culture was universal and could be found in social structures.
* Geertz significantly modified the theories of the mainstream debate, narrowing the dominant concept of culture.

Core Question

In *The Interpretation of Cultures* (1973), Clifford Geertz sought to address anthropology's need to redefine the concept of culture. In doing this, he hoped to reassert the usefulness of anthropology as an academic discipline. Geertz wrote *The Interpretation of Cultures* to offer a new conceptualization of culture as "a system of inherited conceptions expressed in symbolic forms by means of which men communicate, perpetuate, and develop their knowledge about and attitudes toward life."[1] In other words, Geertz wanted to define culture narrowly as the pattern of meaning that can be found in symbols and symbolic action.

Symbols such as a white dove or symbolic actions such as a smile signify ideas and represent qualities that have different, much deeper meaning than the literal meaning of the object or gesture. For example, as a symbol the white dove represents peace; a smile may symbolize the feeling of affection the smiler has for the person he or she smiles at. Symbols change their meanings based on the situation in which they are being used. For instance, a chain can symbolize both "union" and "imprisonment." Therefore, the symbolic meaning of an action or an item hinges on the time, place, and manner in which it is used, and who "reads" it.

Geertz argued that particularly important symbols or rituals reflect a whole culture. For example, Geertz set out to demonstrate that the culture of the Balinese in Indonesia can be understood by comprehending the dynamics of their local ritual of putting on cockfights and betting on the fighting birds. He reports that the Balinese man sees the fighting bird as his "ideal self" and the fight as an arena that represents social tensions. Geertz believed that symbols get their meanings from the roles they play in people's lives, which is why we must study them as phenomena. He believed the main task of anthropologists should be unraveling and interpreting the meanings of symbols.

> "It is to this cutting of the culture concept down to size, therefore actually insuring its continued importance rather than undermining it, that the essays below are all, in their several ways and from their several directions, dedicated."
> —— Clifford Geertz, *The Interpretation of Cultures*

The Participants

Few anthropologists of Geertz's generation agreed about the definition of culture. Geertz's contemporary Roger Keesing,* an influential American cultural anthropologist, identifies four distinct approaches to the "rethinking of culture" in the 1960s.[2]

The first approach viewed culture as interrelated parts that form an overarching structure. The most notable proponent of that approach, the French scholar Claude Lévi-Strauss,* held that many common cultural patterns have their roots in basic structures of the mind. Lévi-Strauss believed that patterns of human thought produce the cultural categories that organize our world views. He argued, for instance, that the human mind has the impulse to categorize opposite concepts, such as light and dark or female and male. According to Lévi-Strauss, these essential conceptual patterns form the foundation for culture. This highly popular structuralist* approach dominated anthropological scholarship at the time.

Second, the American scholars Marshall Sahlins* and Roy Rappaport* proposed ecological approaches that viewed cultures as adaptive systems. An adaptive system, a set of interconnected parts that form a unified whole, responds and adapts to environmental changes. Examples of adaptive systems include natural ecosystems or human communities. Ecological anthropologists* study the relationship between humans and their biophysical environment. They examine how people adapt to their surroundings to survive and maintain themselves.

The third approach to the rethinking of culture at the time held that cultures were cognitive systems (that is, related to people's mental knowledge). Scholars such as Charles Frake* and James Spradley* attempted to formalize a view of culture as patterns of shared knowledge. Cognitive anthropology* examines what people from different groups know, and how that knowledge shapes the way they perceive and relate to the world around them.

The fourth approach to redefining the concept of culture viewed culture as an ensemble of symbolic systems. The pioneers of this approach included Louis Dumont* and Victor Turner* in Europe, and Clifford Geertz and David Schneider* in the United States. Symbolic anthropologists* examined rituals and symbols for their specific cultural meanings. Their studies usually explored the meanings of a particularly significant ritual or symbol, and attempted to show how it reflects an entire culture.

The Contemporary Debate

Geertz argued that cultural context influences the specific meaning of symbols. His concern with "the particular, the circumstantial, the concrete" echoed American anthropologist Franz Boas's* emphasis on particular cultures.[3] Decades earlier, Boas had proposed that anthropologists should research particular cultures and their histories. This contrasted with the then prevailing feeling that anthropologists should attempt to understand the evolution of all humankind.

Geertz acknowledged the relevance of social structures and their functions, as proposed by the European anthropologists Bronisław Malinowski* and Alfred Radcliffe-Brown.* But he distinguished between culture on the one hand and social structure on the other. To Geertz, social structure covers the political, economic, and social relations among people. Culture, on the other hand, signifies the context in which people live.

In *The Interpretation of Cultures*, Geertz most directly took on one of the then key figures in cultural anthropology, the structuralist thinker Claude Lévi-Strauss. Geertz accused Lévi-Strauss of so simplifying complex cultures that he minimized, obscured, and distorted them. Geertz argued that a structuralist approach looked only for schematic relationships. But in his view symbols derive their meanings not from their relationships with each other but from the roles they play in people's lives. Geertz also profoundly disagreed with the structuralist preoccupation with cultural universals that apply everywhere or in all cases. He believed Lévi-Strauss "annuls history, reduces sentiment to a shadow of the intellect, and replaces the particular minds of particular savages in particular jungles with the Savage Mind immanent [inherent] in us all."[4]

---

1. Clifford Geertz, *The Interpretation of Cultures*, 2nd edn (New York: Basic Books, 2000), 89.

2. Roger Keesing, "Theories of Culture," *Annual Review of Anthropology* 3 (1974), 73.

3. Geertz, *The Interpretation of Cultures*, 89.

4. Geertz, *The Interpretation of Cultures*, 355.

MODULE 4
THE AUTHOR'S CONTRIBUTION

KEY POINTS

* In Geertz's view, culture ought to be narrowly defined as the meanings that can be found in the symbolic actions of public life, and subsequently interpreted by means of thick description* (description that explains human behavior in terms of its context, in order to make that behavior meaningful to an outsider).

* The book pointed the way to a new direction in anthropology by advocating an interpretive approach to understanding culture.

* Geertz incorporated and built upon theories from sociology* and the philosophy of language in order to rethink culture.

Author's Aims

Clifford Geertz wrote the essays in *The Interpretation of Cultures* over 15 years. Most had been individually published as he wrote them. In the early 1970s, when Geertz undertook the task of compiling them into a single publication, he decided that "the rendition of culture" had been his "most persistent interest as an anthropologist."[1] Principally, he aimed to put forward "a view of what culture is, what role it plays in social life, and how it ought properly to be studied."[2] So Geertz selected only those essays that directly discussed the concept of culture, and arranged them in "a logical, not a chronological order."[3]

In an introductory chapter to the book, Geertz outlined his

general position and provided an overarching framework for the collection.[4] Generally, he felt an anthropologist can only understand a people's culture by "setting them in the frame of their own banalities," to "expose their normalness without reducing their particularity."[5] Geertz proposed to do this by looking at symbols and symbolic acts—for him, these things represented a culture. He explored what symbolic actions like cockfighting signify for people within a culture—what their "shared meaning is." By doing this, he believed anthropologists can show what such knowledge "demonstrates about the society in which it is found and, beyond that, about social life as such."[6]

For instance, Geertz found that cockfights in the Indonesian province of Bali are not merely entertainment: they cannot be explained by reference to their literal purposes alone. Instead, cockfighting in Bali is a symbolic act: the cocks have metaphorical significance as symbolic representatives of their owners. Balinese men do not engage in cockfighting for the prize money: they do so because a win asserts their social status.

The Balinese remain obsessed with status because they see the cosmos as a grand hierarchy. Derived from Polynesian title ranks and Hindu castes (social classes), this hierarchy places animals and demons at the bottom of the pile and kings and gods at the top. Common humans sit in between those two extremes; a complicated array of ranks assigns a fixed status to everyone. This grand hierarchy forms the moral backbone of Balinese society. Cockfights display (and actualize) the way the Balinese perceive themselves and their social surroundings.

"In anthropology, or anyway social anthropology, what the practitioners do is ethnography. And it is in understanding what ethnography is, or more exactly what doing ethnography is, that a start can be made toward grasping what anthropological analysis amounts to as a form of knowledge."

——Clifford Geertz, *The Interpretation of Cultures*

Approach

Geertz organized the book's 15 essays into five parts that set out the framework for his new way of studying culture. This allowed him to systematically build his argument for an interpretive anthropology.

In the first two parts of his work, Geertz draws on philosophy, literary theory, and sociology. He carefully establishes his theoretical base for defining culture as the meaning embodied in a collection of symbols or clusters of symbolic action. Geertz uses parts three and four of *The Interpretation of Cultures* to examine two specific cultural systems: religion and ideology.

Here, Geertz's focus "shifts from the question of how culture in general provides the human organism with the ordered forms without which it could not think or feel to the question of how specific cultures, in their specific symbolic formations, provide their members with specific systems of meaning and order within which to live their lives."[7] For example, Geertz argued that religion is a specific cultural system, comprising a specific set of symbols. These symbols outline a general order of existence, or the "really real." To Geertz, religious symbols act as vehicles for conceptualizing the "really real." To study them is to bring the particular religion into focus.

Geertz provides a detailed description of the set of symbols that embody a specific cultural system. He also chronicles the behaviors and moods these symbols inspire, and the context within which they have meaning. This level of detail represents what Geertz calls a thick description. This was Geertz's own method of doing ethnography. Thick description allowed him to make explicit the patterns of meaning embodied in a particular set of symbols.

In the fifth and last part of *The Interpretation of Cultures*, Geertz applied his method to interpreting Bali's cultural forms.

In applying thick description to a cultural system, Geertz challenged the then dominant positivist* research tradition. In anthropology, the positivist theory of knowledge views social facts as objects that exist independently of people, the meanings people assign to them, and the action an observer takes in relation to them. Positivist explanations create propositions relating to those objects. These can be verified or proven by means of observation or experiment.

Contribution in Context

Geertz imported the interpretive trend begun by German sociologist Max Weber* into the discipline of anthropology. Weber's concept of *Verstehen** made much of the importance of the meanings that individuals attach to their own actions. The German word *verstehen* means to "understand in a deep way." Researchers arrive at such an in-depth understanding of individuals by putting themselves into the other person's shoes. They do this by interviewing individuals and smaller groups and by experiencing these people's culture directly. This allows the anthropologists to better understand and interpret the meaning within a culture. Previous generations of anthropologists assumed that one set of laws and values could apply to all human experience.

Weber's notion of *Verstehen* critically informed Geertz's attempt to understand cultural meaning from the subjective perspectives of the people whose culture it is[8] (that is, from their point of view, according to their particular context). By adopting Weber's *Verstehen*, Geertz introduced interpretivism* into contemporary anthropology. Interpretivism assumes that we cannot understand people's responses to a situation without knowing how the people themselves see that situation. Geertz's original theory gave *The Interpretation of Cultures* the reputation as "a major voice" of the interpretive anthropology movement of the 1960s.[9]

1. Clifford Geertz, *The Interpretation of Cultures*, 2nd edn (New York: Basic Books 2000), v.

2. Geertz, *The Interpretation of Cultures*, vii.

3. Geertz, *The Interpretation of Cultures*, viii, ix.

4. Geertz, *The Interpretation of Cultures*, ix.

5. Geertz, *The Interpretation of Cultures*, 14.

6. Geertz, *The Interpretation of Cultures*, 26–7.

7. Sherry Ortner, "Clifford Geertz (1926–2006)," *American Anthropologist* 109, no. 4 (2007): 787.

8. Ortner, "Clifford Geertz (1926–2006)," 787.

9. Richard Shweder, "The Resolute Irresolution of Clifford Geertz," *Common Knowledge* 13, nos. 2–3 (Spring-Fall 2007): 191–205.

SECTION 2
IDEAS

MAIN IDEAS

KEY POINTS

* Key themes in *The Interpretation of Cultures* include the nature of culture, the way it operates, and how scholars ought to study it.

* The text chiefly argues that culture resides in symbolic acts. These represent abstract ideas that must be interpreted within their particular social contexts.

* In his main argument Geertz unpicks the principal elements of culture.

Key Themes

In *The Interpretation of Cultures* (1973), Clifford Geertz argues for an understanding of culture as a system of shared meaning: the collective understanding held by members of the same society. As Geertz saw it, every society has symbols and symbolic actions that represent the main tenets of its shared meaning. Every state has a national flag, for example, that symbolizes the country. Such symbols and symbolic actions serve as signifiers, or vehicles, for the shared meaning that characterizes a particular culture. Geertz concluded that anthropologists gain insight into a culture by decoding particularly important symbols and symbolic action, such as myth and ritual. This decoding reveals the meaning that the symbols represent.

Geertz argued that in deciphering the meanings of symbols and symbolic actions anthropologists should read meanings as native people do within their particular social context.

Anthropologists then need to translate and interpret these meanings to outsiders. Geertz explained that anthropologists can only achieve this by immersing themselves in the culture they study. Immersion allows anthropologists to describe in detail the everyday life and practices they observe, and to determine their social ground and import. Geertz termed this particular process of ethnography* thick description.* He took this term from the work of the British philosopher Gilbert Ryle.*

Geertz conceived of thick description as a way of explaining the cultural context of actions, words, and objects and the meaning people place on them. Thick description offers enough context that a person outside the culture can make sense of the behavior. Thin description, by contrast, states facts without such meaning or significance. In *The Interpretation of Cultures*, Geertz proposed anthropologists should consider their principal tasks to be providing thick description and interpreting it to outsiders.[1]

> *"The concept of culture I espouse, and whose utility the essays below attempt to demonstrate, is essentially a semiotic one. Believing, with Max Weber, that man is an animal suspended in webs of significance he himself has spun, I take culture to be those webs, and the analysis of it to be therefore not an experimental science in search of law but an interpretive one in search of meaning."*
> —— Clifford Geertz, *The Interpretation of Cultures*

Exploring the Ideas

Claiming that "man is an animal suspended in webs of significance he himself has spun, [and] I take culture to be those webs," Geertz explained that people shape the patterns of their behaviors and give meaning and significance to their way of life.[2] These meanings, or webs of significance, are the collective property of a group of people—and what we call "culture."

People rely on these shared meanings to sustain their social life. They embody these shared meanings in public symbols and symbolic action so insiders can learn and share them—and outsiders can recognize them. Symbols and symbolic action also transmit meaning, communicating coded messages that help people identify how they should view themselves and others, and how they should feel about the world.

By focusing on the central role of symbols and symbolic action in capturing, carrying, and transmitting the web of shared meaning we call culture, Geertz put forward a semiotic* concept of culture—one rooted in signs and symbols that epitomize the abstract ideas they stand for. Geertz's semiotic concept of culture saw that the meaning of a symbol is not set in stone. It can vary based on the context and the motivation of the person who acts.

Given this, Geertz argued that the anthropologist must spell out "the implicit or unstated presuppositions, implications, or meaning that make this or that action, practice, object, or pattern of sounds intelligible to members of some culture or interpretive community in some specific context."[3] In other words, the anthropologist unravels the web of meaning that a symbol or symbolic action presents within a particular context, and then translates and conveys it to outsiders.

According to Geertz, this task is much like trying to read an ensemble of texts with the anthropologist straining "to read over the shoulders of those to whom [these texts] properly belong."[4] To him, interpreting "culture as text" constituted the very essence of thick description. The English philosopher of language Gilbert Ryle identified a difference between a "thick description" that takes account of the circumstances, and a "thin description" that has no context.[5]

Ryle gives the example of someone "rapidly raising and lowering their right eyelid"—the physical act of winking. The person could suffer from an uncontrollable twitch; he or she could have done it on purpose in order to interact with someone else, for example to catch their attention; or the person could have winked in order to make fun of someone with a nervous twitch. It all hinges on the circumstances and the intentions of the individual who is winking. This implies that communication, description, and explanation cannot clearly be separated. All except the most trivial descriptions of human actions and behavior involve interpretations, expectations, and explanations of why people acted the way they did and what they were seeking to achieve in doing so. Geertz argues, in essence, that we must pay attention to the *full* meaning of people's actions before we can believe we understand them.

Language and Expression

Geertz set out his treatise systematically by arguing "sometimes explicitly, more often merely through the particular analysis ...

for a narrowed, specialized, and ... theoretically more powerful concept of culture."[6] To that end, the essays in *The Interpretation of Cultures* first defined culture, then examined two specific cultural systems, and finally applied Geertz's method of thick description to interpreting a particular ritual.

Despite the author's effort to be systematic, critics have found *The Interpretation of Cultures* complex and somewhat difficult to follow. Geertz's entertaining and poetic writing style does not help. It tends to be stylistically peculiar, putting its point across in metaphors and anecdotes as opposed to simple explanations. In fact, one critic, referencing a nineteenth-century English novelist, described Geertz as the "Jane Austen* of ethnography."[7] The American philosopher Richard Rorty* described Geertz's writing as "self-conscious exhibitions and commentaries on the very process of thought."[8]

As a result, general-interest readers have frequently misunderstood and misinterpreted *The Interpretation of Cultures*. Geertz's student Sherry Ortner* noted that one obituary described Geertz's ideas as "covered in fuzz" and bemoaned that he turned anthropology "into a lame and confused form of literary scholarship."[9]

1. Richard Shweder, "Clifford Geertz," *Proceedings of the American Philosophical Society* 154, no. 1 (March 2010): 90.

2. Clifford Geertz, *The Interpretation of Cultures*, 2nd edn (New York: Basic Books, 2000), 5.

3. Geertz, *The Interpretation of Cultures*, 10.

4. Geertz, *The Interpretation of Cultures*, 452.

5. Gilbert Ryle, *The Concept of Mind* (Chicago: University of Chicago Press, 1949).

6. Geertz, *The Interpretation of Cultures*, viii.

7. Renato Rosaldo Jr., "Geertz's Gifts," *Common Knowledge* 13, nos. 2–3 (2007): 208.

8. Richard Shweder and Byron Good, eds., *Clifford Geertz by His Colleagues* (Chicago: University of Chicago Press, 2005), 50.

9. Sherry Ortner, "Clifford Geertz (1926–2006)," *American Anthropologist* 109, no. 4 (2007): 788.

SECONDARY IDEAS

KEY POINTS

- Geertz's two main secondary ideas involve his interpretations of religion and ideology as cultural systems.

- Geertz was far ahead of his time with his theories on religion and ideology as specific systems of meaning.

- With today's societies becoming more divided along religious and ideological lines, Geertz's theories still have much to contribute to current debates.

Other Ideas

Clifford Geertz's *The Interpretation of Cultures* contains two significant secondary ideas—religion and ideology as two specific "meaning systems." Geertz used these to illustrate his core thesis.

Geertz shows how both religion and ideology provide people with particular systems of meaning and help them order their lives.[1] Religion, he proposes, is a cultural system devoted to defining what is "really real" for people;[2] it is a set of symbols that creates compelling and enduring feelings in people by setting out a general order of existence: the way things are, on both the cosmic and material level. These conceptions were clothed with factuality—that is, they were presented as facts; in this way, the feelings created by the system of symbols were made to appear uniquely real and tangible.[3]

Geertz examined ideology the same way. He claimed that, just like religion, it serves as "an ordered system of cultural symbols" that establishes directions to help people find their way.[4] People use ideology's symbolic systems to express political faith in a set of ideas; these ideas might concern social arrangements, institutional power, organizational frameworks, and governing elites. Geertz notes that people embrace an ideological "meaning system" to ease their tensions. These tensions may stem from, among other things, watching the world or losing social and political orientation. Ideologies appeal to our emotional desire to believe in larger-than-life possibilities. They serve as both an expression of our hope and a reflection of our despair.

Geertz illuminated his argument by interpreting ideological developments in the 66 countries that achieved political independence from colonial rule between 1945 and 1968. He demonstrated how ideological parties manipulated the meaning of symbols according to the needs of a particular society and the demands of its historical situation.

> "To look at the symbolic dimensions of social action—art, religion, ideology, science, law, morality, common sense— is not to turn away from the existential dilemmas of life for some empyrean* realm of de-emotionalized forms; it is to plunge into the midst of them."
> ——Clifford Geertz, *The Interpretation of Cultures*

Exploring the Ideas

Geertz argued that, in a world in which man's life has "no genuine order at all—no empirical regularity, no emotional form, no moral coherence," religion serves as a central cultural system to reassure people. Through its symbols, religion presents "an image of ... a genuine order of the world, which will account for, and even celebrate, the perceived ambiguities, puzzles, and paradoxes."5 In other words, Geertz suggests religion exists to comfort people and assure them that everything has an order.

To achieve this, "sacred symbols function to synthesize a people's ethos ... and their world view."6 At its heart, then, a religious perspective enables people to feel a connection between how life should be (as specified by the religion in question) and the way things really are.

Geertz illustrated this point by discussing the funeral of a young boy in Java who had died suddenly. The ritual failed to achieve its purpose of producing *iklas*,* acceptance of death, and *rukun*,* communal harmony. Instead, it stoked communal tension. Geertz considered that the funeral rites failed for several reasons.

The first reason for this failure was that, because of conflict between a local official and the political party with which the boy's family was affiliated, the community did not follow the usual Islamic procedures. The second reason involved improvised modifications created to allow the funeral to proceed; instead of coming to a collective consensus about ways to alter the funeral rite, one individual took charge and made the changes unilaterally. The conflict that arose at the funeral, in Geertz's view, stemmed from a burgeoning gap between the community's cultural beliefs and social interaction in real life.

Geertz saw the role of ideology as "justificatory" and "apologetic": it establishes and defends patterns of belief and value.7

To Geertz, ideologies seek only selective questions and answers, and target only narrow problems. That leads them to underestimate or exaggerate social realities. For example, the widespread ideology of anti-Semitism*—hostility toward Jewish people—in Europe of the 1930s and 1940s placed the blame for social and economic problems on one target enemy: Jews. Geertz advocated an analytical framework to examine ideologies as something other than weapons that different interests use in an ongoing struggle for power. He observed that the term "ideology" had taken on an "evaluative" connotation, which made it into a diagnosis of social, political, and intellectual diseases that diverted societies from a sensible appreciation of reality.

In the aftermath of the World War II,* and in the midst of the long period of global tension known as the Cold War* and the political turmoil that followed the end of the colonial period in many nations, particularly in Africa, Asia, and the Caribbean, Geertz sensed that ideology actually "draws its persuasive power from any discrepancy between what is believed and what can, now or someday, be established as scientifically correct."[8] Accordingly, he noted that the social sciences needed to develop a "genuinely non-evaluative conception of ideology" (a conception that does not seek to establish the soundness of any ideology), capable of taking social and psychological contexts into account.[9] This proposition offered a route to defining "ideology" in a way that social scientists in general could find useful.

Overlooked

Despite the dense and complex argument Geertz puts forward in

The Interpretation of Cultures, we may argue that all significant aspects have been examined and discussed. Many scholars have offered their differing perspectives on one aspect or another of the book in the past 40 years. Indeed, as one reviewer puts it, "to criticize Geertz has become an anthropological obsession, almost a rite of passage."[10]

Scholars have focused their attention on many things. These include the volume's view of culture as intrinsic to evolution, its theory on particular "meaning systems," its method of thick description,* its regional focus and ethnographies,* its neglect of important modern concepts and theories, its implications for disciplines beyond anthropology, its deliberation of issues of social and moral philosophy, and even its literary flair.[11]

Reconsidering the text against the background of contemporary political events, social problems, and historical developments may yield new and interesting insights. But it will not significantly change the way in which we understand *The Interpretation of Cultures* as a whole. For this same reason, Geertz chose not to change anything of substance to improve or update his arguments before publication in 1973—more than a decade after he wrote the essays. And certainly much had happened in the world and in anthropology by the time he republished the work in 2000. Yet still he made no substantive changes. As Geertz put it, "some of the hares I started then have turned out to be worth chasing."[12]

1. Sherry Ortner, "Clifford Geertz (1926–2006)," *American Anthropologist* 109, no. 4 (2007): 787.
2. Clifford Geertz, *The Interpretation of Cultures*, 2nd edn (New York: Basic Books, 2000), 112.
3. Geertz, *The Interpretation of Cultures*, 90.
4. Geertz, *The Interpretation of Cultures*, 196.
5. Geertz, *The Interpretation of Cultures*, 107–8.
6. Geertz, *The Interpretation of Cultures*, 89.
7. Geertz, *The Interpretation of Cultures*, 231.
8. Geertz, *The Interpretation of Cultures*, 72.
9. Geertz, *The Interpretation of Cultures*, 196.
10. E. Bruner, "Book Review: Clifford Geertz: His Critics and Followers, 1998," *Anthropology and Humanism* 23, no. 2 (1998): 216.
11. Ortner, "Clifford Geertz (1926–2006)," 787.
12. Geertz, *The Interpretation of Cultures*, vi.

ACHIEVEMENT

KEY POINTS

* Geertz successfully set out a "treatise in cultural theory."
* The publication of *The Interpretation of Cultures* coincided neatly with anthropology's need to reinvent itself as a discipline.
* *The Interpretation of Cultures* remains relevant across place, time, and cultures, both in and beyond the discipline of anthropology.

Assessing the Argument

In the early 1970s, Clifford Geertz's publisher asked him to select a set of his essays and arrange them into the book that would become *The Interpretation of Cultures*. At first, he remained unsure about what his intention should be. Most of the essays resulting from several years of fieldwork in Indonesia fell into the category Geertz called "empirical studies" (that is, studies based on information verifiable by observation). He eventually decided to include all his essays that "bear, directly and explicitly, on the concept of culture" and how to study such a concept.[1] He wanted to share with the world his definition of culture as webs of meaning as well as his interpretive* approach to studying these webs.

To do this, he had to explain and translate the subjective and contextual meanings of the people whose culture it is. Geertz felt that "it is in understanding what ethnography* is, or more exactly what doing ethnography is, that a start can be made toward grasping what anthropological analysis amounts to as a form of knowledge"[2] ("ethnography" refers to research exploring cultural phenomena, documented in written field studies or case studies). In showcasing the scientific knowledge his interpretive study of culture produced, Geertz also wanted to highlight the relevance of anthropology as a discipline.

It is fair to say that the argument Geertz put forward in *The Interpretation of Cultures* achieved its goal. The volume's call to understand the human condition "as defined by the constant production and transformation of meaning" proved critical to the evolution of the intellectual environment.[3] It caused a fundamental shift in the discipline's aims and methods often referred to as the "interpretive turn" in anthropology.[4] Geertz's "treatise in cultural theory" not only offered a new definition of culture (the central, unifying concept of anthropology as it was practiced in the United States) but also successfully established that we ought to study culture by interpreting the subjective meanings that people in any given culture ascribe to their social action.

Geertz's collection of essays also succeeded in challenging the then dominant idea of culture as universal and all-encompassing. It called into question the value of positivist* approaches to studying culture, which maintained that social facts exist independent of people and their meanings. It also presented an alternative to structuralist* and functionalist* approaches, both of which looked only at meaning embedded in structures; functionalist approaches consider all aspects of social and cultural behavior to be "organs," so to speak, serving some vital function in the "organism" of a society. Geertz's method of thick description* came to define not only his method of ethnography but also those of cultural anthropologists in general.

> "Certain ideas burst upon the intellectual landscape with a tremendous force. They resolve so many fundamental problems at once that they seem also to promise that they will resolve all fundamental problems, clarify all obscure issues."
>
> ——Clifford Geertz, *The Interpretation of Cultures*

Achievement in Context

The Interpretation of Cultures hit bookstores as anthropology struggled to reinvent itself as a discipline. Practitioners had begun to question and rethink the core concept of culture put forward by previous generations. Geertz's ideas shaped the new definition of American cultural anthropology.

The Interpretation of Cultures did much to cement cultural anthropology as a respected and valued subdivision of anthropology in its own right. It separated the discipline from biological anthropology* (the study of human evolution), linguistic anthropology* (the study of language and how it represents culture), and archaeological anthropology* (the study of the historical traces of human culture) in the United States, and from social anthropology* (the study of social structures and their role in human cultures) in the United Kingdom. It gave cultural anthropology a rationale for the era following the end of the colonial period* and inspired the growth of modern cultural comparative studies—studies that seek to understand cultures by examining their differences and similarities.

The book had its most direct impact on the wider intellectual environment as a proponent of an interpretive movement in anthropology. Many scholars remained unconvinced by Geertz's exclusive emphasis on symbols. But they considered *The Interpretation of Cultures* to be the reference for interpretive inquiry. A seminal book, it influenced ideas about theory and method across many academic disciplines. The most influential social science books frequently cited it. Translated into 20 languages, the work has turned Geertz into "a true giant of social and cultural theory."[5]

Limitations

Today we grapple with social problems such as cyberbullying* and global warming* that Geertz could not have foreseen when he wrote *The Interpretation of Cultures* 40 years ago. This "limitation" is, perhaps, inevitable. For his "treatise in culture" Geertz typically studied static, small-scale, homogeneous (internally similar), and relatively isolated societies.[6] By contrast, modern cultures are fluid and characterized by a lack of unity. The identities and subjectivities*—interpretations of experience that differ according to our various identities—dissolve in the many webs of meaning that make up every present-day culture; men, women, Muslims, Buddhists, drug addicts, teetotalers, homosexuals, heterosexuals, bisexuals (to name just a few) contribute differently to the formation of these many webs of meaning.

Today people consider themselves part of multiple cultures.

They may share a culture with their particular ethnic group, the country they live in, the organization they work for, their social class, their religious community, or their virtual friends*—the list can go on and on. In today's world culture is neither bounded nor isolated. Any one person can be just as much part of any particular culture as he or she would like. People have internalized an assemblage of different meaning fragments from a range of cultures, or meaning systems, at any point in time.[7] This makes "culture" even more difficult to define than it was when Geertz wrote this work.

---

1. Clifford Geertz, *The Interpretation of Cultures*, 2nd edn (New York: Basic Books, 2000), vii.
2. Geertz, *The Interpretation of Cultures*, 5–6.
3. Sherry Ortner, "Clifford Geertz (1926–2006)," *American Anthropologist* 109, no. 4 (2007): 787.
4. Sherry Ortner, "Special Issue: The Fate of 'Culture': Geertz and beyond," *Representations* 59 (1997): 6.
5. Jeffrey Alexander et al., eds., *Interpreting Clifford Geertz: Cultural Investigation in the Social Sciences* (New York: Palgrave Macmillan, 2011), xiii.
6. Geertz, *The Interpretation of Cultures*, viii.
7. David Kronenfeld et al., eds., *A Companion to Cognitive Anthropology* (Singapore: Blackwell Publishing Ltd., 2011).

MODULE 8
PLACE IN THE AUTHOR'S WORK

KEY POINTS

* The chief focus of Geertz's life's work has been the rendition,* or translation, of culture.
* Considered a masterwork, *The Interpretation of Cultures* became Geertz's best-known publication.
* *The Interpretation of Cultures* established Geertz as one of the founding fathers of the interpretive* or symbolic movement.

Positioning

Before Clifford Geertz collected his essays and published them as *The Interpretation of Cultures*, he spent 10 years as professor of anthropology at the University of Chicago. In this period, from 1960 to 1970, Geertz focused his research on two Indonesian* islands, Java and Bali, resulting in three books: *The Religion of Java* (1960), *Agricultural Involution* (1963), and *Peddlers and Princes* (also 1963).[1] During the sixties, Geertz conducted research in Morocco, and his work produced a number of publications, including a book in which he compares Indonesia and Morocco, entitled *Islam Observed* (1968).[2]

Geertz published *The Interpretation of Cultures* after taking a position as professor of social science at the Institute for Advanced Study at Princeton University. The book contained a selection of essays that Geertz had individually published throughout the sixties. Geertz purposely chose not to create a publication that would be a "review or autobiography of his career."[3] Instead, he looked to find a through-line in his work. As he combed through his essays, he decided that "the rendition [interpretation] of culture" had been his "most persistent interest as an anthropologist."[4]

Although Geertz had changed his intellectual standpoint slightly over the years, he resisted the temptation to write his "changed view back into earlier works"[5] and left the essays' central arguments untouched. When the book, originally published in 1973, was reissued in 2000, the only substantive thing Geertz added to the original edition was an introductory chapter. This introduction outlined his general position and provided an overarching framework for the collection.[6]

⌐ *"Whether [Geertz] is revered or reviled, all those involved in cultural research have to be familiar with his work, just as all psychoanalytic thinkers must deal with Freud,* all critical theorists with Marx, and all structuralists* with Saussure.*"*
—— Jeffrey Alexander et al., *Interpreting Clifford Geertz: Cultural Investigation in the Social Sciences* ⌐

Integration

The Interpretation of Cultures became Geertz's best-known publication, establishing him as one of the founding fathers of the interpretive or symbolic movement. In 1974 he further cemented this reputation by editing the anthology *Myth, Symbol, and Culture.*[7] That collection contained papers on symbolic anthropology* by a number of important anthropologists. During this period, Geertz also published ethnographic* studies, such as *Kinship in Bali* (1975) and—together with Hildred Geertz and Lawrence Rosen—*Meaning and Order in Moroccan Society* (1979).[8]

From the 1980s onward, Geertz published theoretical essays and reviews for the *New York Review of Books*. The books that he wrote during this period featured collected essays, including *Local Knowledge* (1983), *Available Light* (2000), and *Life Among The Anthros* (published posthumously in 2010).[9] He also published a volume with short essays on the method of ethnography, which was entitled *Works and Lives* (1988), as well as the autobiography *After the Fact* (1995).[10]

While we may certainly consider Geertz's body of work coherent, his views evolved during his long career. Critics argue that his intellectual journey charts three broad trends.[11] First, Geertz became increasingly convinced that no knowledge is universal. Instead, he determined that insights only hold true for a particular group of individuals. Second, Geertz became less worried about functionalism* (roughly, interpreting a culture by considering the useful "functions" that its various parts serve) and increasingly concerned with the need to study culture in semiotic* terms (that is, by interpreting symbols and language). Third, Geertz always grounded his approach in discrete, specific "cultural portraits." But it began to seem imperative to him "to think [more] in terms of 'cultures' (lowercase and multiple) than 'Culture' (capitalized and singular)."[12]

Significance

Geertz's body of work has influenced scholars from a range of disciplines. He had a profound impact on theory and method in anthropology, and in the fields of history, sociology,* religious studies, and cultural studies. Some joke that Geertz became so famous that he generated his own "cultural system."[13] The "Geertz culture" ties together key terms, such as thick description,* and frequently repeated quotes, images, and parables from his body of work. Critics argue that such reference capable of generating instantaneous recognition is found only very rarely and with the most influential thinkers, such as the pioneering sociologist Max Weber* and the notably influential political philosopher Karl Marx.*[14]

Lists of the most influential science books routinely cite Geertz's masterwork *The Interpretation of Cultures* alongside the French sociologist and anthropologist Pierre Bourdieu's* book *Distinction* and the American sociologist C. Wright Mills's* *The Sociological Imagination.*[15] In addition, *The Interpretation of Cultures* boasts an Amazon.com sales ranking of 8000, even though it first appeared more than 40 years ago, back when "Amazon" was merely a river.[16]

Interpretive or symbolic anthropology has proven to be a popular and influential school of thought within and beyond the discipline of anthropology. It remains as central to modern debates about globalization (the trend toward increasingly close cultural, economic, and political ties across continental boundaries) and cultural pluralism (the coexistence of several cultures in the same society) as it was 40 years ago to the debates on cultural appropriation (the acquisition of cultural habits, usually by a "dominant" culture).[17]

1. Clifford Geertz, *The Religion of Java* (Glencoe: The Free Press, *1960*); *Agricultural Involution: The Processes of Ecological Change in Indonesia* (Los Angeles: University of California Press, 1963); *Peddlers and Princes: Social Development and Economic Change in Two Indonesian Towns* (Chicago: University of Chicago Press, 1963).

2. Clifford Geertz, *Islam Observed: Religious Development in Morocco and Indonesia* (New Haven: Yale University Press, 1968).

3. Clifford Geertz, *The Interpretation of Cultures,* 2nd edn (New York: Basic Books, 2000), viii.

4. Geertz, *The Interpretation of Cultures*, v.

5. Geertz, *The Interpretation of Cultures*, viii.

6. Geertz, *The Interpretation of Cultures*, ix.

7. Clifford Geertz, ed., *Myth, Symbol, and Culture* (New York: Norton, 1974).

8. Clifford Geertz, *Kinship in Bali* (Chicago: University of Chicago Press, 1975) and Clifford Geertz, Hildred Geertz, and Lawrence Rosen, *Meaning and Order in Moroccan Society* (New York: Cambridge University Press, 1979).

9. Clifford Geertz, *Local Knowledge: Further Essays in Interpretive Anthropology* (New York: Basic Books, 1983); *Available Light: Anthropological Reflections on Philosophical Topics* (Princeton: Princeton University Press, 2000); *Life among the Anthros and Other Essays* (Princeton: Princeton University Press, 2010).

10. Clifford Geertz, *Works and Lives: The Anthropologist as Author* (Stanford: Stanford University Press, 1988); *After the Fact: Two Countries, Four Decades, One Anthropologist* (Cambridge, MA: Harvard University Press, 1995).

11. Aram Yengoyan, "Clifford Geertz, Cultural Portraits, and Southeast Asia," *The Journal of Asian Studies* 68, no. 4 (November 2009): 1215–16.

12. Yengoyan, "Clifford Geertz," 1216.

13. Jeffrey Alexander et al., eds., *Interpreting Clifford Geertz: Cultural Investigation in the Social Sciences* (New York: Palgrave Macmillan, 2011), xiii–xiv.

14. Alexander et al., eds., *Interpreting Clifford Geertz,* xiii–xiv.

15. Alexander et al., eds., *Interpreting Clifford Geertz,* xiii–xiv. See Pierre Bourdieu, *Distinction: A Social Critique of the Judgement of Taste,* translated by Richard Nice (Cambridge, MA: Harvard University Press, 1987) and C. Wright Mills, *The Sociological Imagination* (New York: Oxford University Press, 1959).

16. Alexander et al., eds., *Interpreting Clifford Geertz,* xiv.

17. Sherry Ortner, "Special Issue: The Fate of 'Culture': Geertz and beyond," *Representations* 59 (1997): 1–14.

SECTION 3
IMPACT

THE FIRST RESPONSES

KEY POINTS

* The main criticism of Geertz's *The Interpretation of Cultures* revolved around the author's subjective interpretive* approach (his method of interpreting cultural features, as understood by the people that made up his cultural study, for outsiders), his focus on symbols, and his neglect of power, conflict, inequality, and historical processes.

* Addressing his critics, Geertz could only emphasize his different view on the nature of social life and the prospects of creating rules to explain human behavior.

* Scholars consider Geertz's work a productive place to start learning about an interpretive approach to culture.

Criticism

When Geertz published *The Interpretation of Cultures*, positivism* dominated the research tradition in anthropology. The positivist theory of knowledge holds that social facts exist independently of people and the contextual meanings people give to these facts. We can verify or prove these facts by means of observation or experiment. Positivist scholars argued that Geertz took an unscientific approach to culture. They felt he relied too much on interpretation, which led to "uncontrolled subjectivism"[1]—that is, his findings had more to do with his own understanding than with objective, verifiable "truth."

Even anthropologists who understood the benefits of an

interpretive approach criticized *The Interpretation of Cultures*. They felt Geertz had invested in too narrow a semiotic* concept of culture—a concept that relies on the reading of meanings in signs and symbols. For instance, some of Geertz's influential contemporaries opposed his symbolic approaches. Anthropologists such as Marvin Harris,* Roy Rappaport,* Marshall Sahlins,* and Andrew P. Vayda* argued instead that we should understand culture as a non-biological means humans use to adapt to life in different environments. Maintaining that all cultural phenomena arise in response to the practical problems of life on earth, these anthropologists criticized Geertz for neglecting power, conflict, and inequality. They also objected to his political and ethical neutrality.[2] For instance, when the anthropologist Talal Asad* examined Geertz's definition of religion, he found "it omits the crucial dimension of power" and "ignores the varying social conditions for the production of knowledge."[3]

Scholars of all convictions took issue with the explanatory reach of Geertz's seminal work. They pointed out "the explanation was based solely on the depth and detail of the description." In other words, Geertz had let culture describe and explain itself.[4] For instance, historians argued that Geertz's explanation of a system of meaning typically failed to consider "the historical processes that led to its production."[5] Talal Asad echoed this claim. He ended his critical evaluation of Geertz's account of religion with the plea to investigate religion "with reference to the historical conditions necessary for the existence of particular practices and discourses."[6]

> *"Indeed, to criticize Geertz has become an anthropological obsession, almost a rite of passage."*
>
> —— Edward Bruner, "Book Review: Clifford Geertz: His Critics and Followers, 1998"

Responses

Geertz never joined the scientific debates among anthropologists and did not make much effort to defend his work against critics. He justified his silence by reasoning that his main interest was to articulate "a positive program for anthropology."[7]

When pressed, he could only emphasize his different view on "the character of social life and the prospects of developing law-like explanatory statements about human behavior."[8] Geertz did not see human culture as a power "to which social events, behaviors, institutions, or processes can be causally attributed" by identifying schematic relationships and cultural universals.[9] Instead, Geertz understood culture as a context within which particular individuals construct systems of meaning. He stressed that "the whole point of a semiotic approach to culture is to aid us in gaining access to the conceptual world in which our subjects live so that we can, in some extended sense of the term, converse with them."[10]

Geertz also explained that most of the meanings that determine human behavior remain narrow in scope, limited to a particular local context. So he reasoned that social science generalizations will inevitably also be restricted in scope.[11] In his later work, Geertz further deepened his commitment to studying culture in a particularistic* and relativistic* way—that is, by considering every culture as a "particular" (singular) case in which beliefs, practices, and so on have no greater or lesser claim to validity or worth than those of any other culture (notably that of the anthropologist).

Conflict and Consensus

Many anthropologists remained unconvinced by Clifford Geertz's exclusive emphasis on symbols. But they considered it a sound starting point for an interpretive approach to culture, which needs to be supplemented by also considering other aspects that define a culture, such as history, power dynamics, and social structures, among other things.[12]

Significant consensus had formed around the importance of interpreting meaning from the acting person's subjective point of view. Questioning the then common positivist model, many agreed with Geertz's argument that it remains important to understand meaning based on context and the intention of the person who acts in specific situations. For that reason, scholars still see *The Interpretation of Cultures* as a powerful resource for those who want to go beyond positivist* data collection or grand structural* theories (theories that assume that a culture can be analyzed by identifying the relationship between the elements that compose its structure). Scholars find value in the book's proposition that anthropologists must study how people make sense of the world around them.

Despite its critics, *The Interpretation of Cultures* defined the central ideas of the discipline of American cultural anthropology.* That seems a powerful indicator of the consensus that the book generated. Geertz's work distinguished cultural anthropology from closely related approaches such as social anthropology,* which studies relationships between humans. It gave anthropology a new justification in the postcolonial* era. It also inspired the growth of the modern discipline of cultural comparative studies.

1. Sherry Ortner, "Special Issue: The Fate of 'Culture': Geertz and beyond," *Representations* 59 (1997), 1–14.
2. Edward Bruner, "Book Review: Clifford Geertz: His Critics and Followers, 1998," *Anthropology and Humanism* 23, no. 2 (1998): 216.
3. Talal Asad, "Anthropological Conceptions of Religion: Reflections on Geertz," *Man* 18, no. 2 (1983): 237–59.
4. Aram Yengoyan, "Clifford Geertz, Cultural Portraits, and Southeast Asia," *The Journal of Asian Studies* 68, no. 4 (November 2009): 1217.
5. Bruner, "Book Review: Clifford Geertz: His Critics and Followers, 1998," 216.
6. Asad, "Anthropological Conceptions of Religion," 237.
7. Sherry Ortner, "Clifford Geertz (1926–2006)," *American Anthropologist* 109, no. 4 (2007): 788.
8. Richard Shweder, "The Resolute Irresolution of Clifford Geertz," *Common Knowledge* 13, nos. 2–3 (Spring-Fall 2007), 197.
9. Clifford Geertz, *The Interpretation of Cultures*, 2nd edn (New York: Basic Books, 2000), 14.
10. Geertz, *The Interpretation of Cultures*, 24.
11. Shweder, "The Resolute Irresolution of Clifford Geertz," 196.
12. Bruner, "Book Review: Clifford Geertz: His Critics and Followers, 1998," 216.

MODULE 10
THE EVOLVING DEBATE

KEY POINTS

- Geertz's relativist* approach—his theoretical stand that no culture's beliefs and practices could lay claim to any particular validity—and his interpretation of alternative moral universes (other systems of morality) appealed to many scholars.

- Many credit *The Interpretation of Cultures* with popularizing an interpretive* school of thought.

- While cultural anthropologists* share an affinity for Geertz's interpretivism, they do not view cultures as bounded and isolated. So they supplement Geertz's approach by looking at wider political, economic, social, historical, and cultural frameworks that affect the ways in which local people assign meanings within their culture.

Uses and Problems

While many scholars remained unconvinced by Clifford Geertz's exclusive emphasis on symbols as codes for cultural meaning, the ideas he put forward in *The Interpretation of Cultures* proved very popular. In fact, scholars credit them with popularizing an interpretive school of thought. They have also affected the direction of thinking in a huge variety of disciplines.

Drawing on the aims and methods of several disciplines, Geertz took an interdisciplinary* approach to his work. His theories on culture as systems of meaning had relevance for sociology,* religious studies, psychology, philosophy, and other humanist sciences. They have also intrigued scholars in the disciplines of communication studies, geography, ecology, political science, comparative legal studies, history, and literary criticism.[1] His insistence on the distinctiveness of the subjective and contextual* world views of people attracted scholarly attention—as did his interpretive approach to unraveling these world views. Richard Shweder,* another noted American cultural anthropologist, explained that *The Interpretation of Cultures* offers a "provocative" yet "portable" set of beliefs. These have widely appealed to scholars across disciplines.

To many of these scholars Geertz's method remains less important than his cultural pluralism—his way of considering different cultures on their own terms, a notion central to his relativist approach. It also informs his interpretation of alternative moral universes (the idea that there is not an essential human "morality" applicable to all people at all times).[2] Thinkers from other disciplines commonly adapted Geertz's belief "that diversity is inherent to the human condition; that there is no universal essence to human nature." They have also agreed "that the ... impulse to value uniformity (convergence in belief) over variety, and to overlook, devalue, or seek to eradicate 'difference,' is not a good thing."[3]

> *"The results suggest that although we can move beyond Geertz, we can never leave him behind."*
> ——Jeffrey Alexander et al., *Interpreting Clifford Geertz: Cultural Investigation in the Social Sciences*

Schools of Thought

By mapping out his particular approach to the analysis of culture, Geertz charted a new direction in anthropological theory and method. He made it contextual and interpretive in nature.[4] In fact, Geertz helped to establish a new school of thought, called "interpretive or symbolic anthropology."* He based this approach to understanding humans and societies on systematically unraveling webs of subjective world views.[5] Interpretive anthropology turned scholars' attention toward issues of culture and interpretation. This may be its most significant accomplishment. Previously, anthropologists had focused almost exclusively on developing grand theories.

Interpretive anthropology arose as a direct reaction to then popular schools of thought such as materialism* and Marxism*— related approaches to understanding history and society that emphasize material factors such as economics and social class. (The materialist school defined culture as consisting only of observable behaviors, while, for Marxists, material factors such as economics and social class are the principle drivers of history.) The school that came to be known as symbolic or interpretive anthropology contributed to the subsequent development of modern schools of thought in the social sciences. It also established how important it is to consider the effect the personality or presence of the researcher has on what he or she investigates.[6]

Other important cultural anthropologists associated with interpretive anthropology include Marshall Sahlins,* David

Schneider,* Victor Turner,* and Mary Douglas.* Many consider Geertz and these four prominent scholars as the founders of symbolic or interpretive anthropology.

In Current Scholarship

Clifford Geertz spent the majority of his career doing ethnography* in remote places.[7] He directly supervised only a small number of PhD candidates, but during his 30–year tenure at Princeton's Institute for Advanced Study, Geertz influenced hundreds of social scientists and historians through fellowships, seminars, and lunch conversations.[8]

Whatever discipline they come from, scholars who support and promote *The Interpretation of Cultures* share an affinity for Geertz's interpretivism, his concept of culture, his relativism and particularism* (his belief that every culture should be understood according to the values that it holds, and is a product of its particular historical and environmental context), his intellectual cross-fertilization, and his literary flair. They also appreciate his insistence that we need to understand better the process of understanding.[9] Above all, they feel in harmony with Geertz's call to study human diversity in its plurality.

In their own work Geertz's supporters seem to focus on the issue of making meaning as opposed to the notion of cultural systems.[10] We see this particularly in Geertz's own field of anthropology. Many modern ethnographers continue to study the distinct ways in which people in different localities experience their lives. This group includes Sherry Ortner,* Lila Abu-Lughod,*

George Marcus,* and Renato Rosaldo Jr.* Unlike Geertz, however, these practitioners do not view cultures as bounded and isolated. They supplement Geertz's approach by looking at the wider political, economic, social, historical, and cultural frameworks that affect local meaning-making.[11] Geertz's most visible, outspoken, and prominent disciples may be the cultural anthropologists Sherry Ortner, who studied with him, and Richard Shweder.* Both have conducted award-winning academic research.

---

1. See Sherry Ortner, "Special Issue: The Fate of 'Culture': Geertz and beyond," *Representations* 59 (1997): 1–14; and Richard Shweder, "The Resolute Irresolution of Clifford Geertz," *Common Knowledge* 13, nos. 2–3 (Spring-Fall 2007): 191–205.

2. Richard Shweder and Byron Good, eds., *Clifford Geertz by His Colleagues* (Chicago: University of Chicago Press, 2005), 8.

3. Ortner, "Special Issue," 1–14.

4. Sherry Ortner, "Clifford Geertz (1926–2006)," *American Anthropologist* 109, no. 4 (2007), 789.

5. Ortner, "Clifford Geertz (1926–2006)," 787.

6. Ortner, "Clifford Geertz (1926–2006)," 787.

7. Ortner, "Clifford Geertz (1926–2006)," 788.

8. Ortner, "Clifford Geertz (1926–2006)," 787.

9. Shweder and Good, *Clifford Geertz by His Colleagues,* 9.

10. Ortner, "Special Issue," 1.

11. Ortner, "Special Issue," 1–14.

IMPACT AND INFLUENCE TODAY

KEY POINTS

* *The Interpretation of Cultures* is one of a body of revered works for anthropologists practicing interpretive* scholarship.
* Although these scholars have widely adopted Geertz's "interpretive turn," the general consensus remains that anthropologists need to supplement the Geertzian concept of culture for it to be relevant in the modern world.
* Following Geertz, anthropologists need to reconfigure the concept of culture for an increasingly interdependent, complex, and ever-changing world.

Position

Some 40 years after its initial publication, Clifford Geertz's *The Interpretation of Cultures* has become part of a "sacred canon."[1] Today, it forms part of the essential reading list for anyone interested in interpretive approaches in the social sciences and humanities.

Scholars generally agree that they need to complement the Geertzian concept of culture with additional research looking at wider political, economic, social, and historical conditions. But the relevance of *The Interpretation of Cultures* has not diminished.[2] The discipline has widely adopted Geertz's so-called "interpretive turn." To this day it remains the approach taken by many cultural and social anthropologists.* Historians, sociologists,* political scientists, and scholars of other disciplines who collect ethnographic* data in their research projects also use Geertz's approach.[3] They share with him the interpretive method of teasing out and analyzing the meanings of texts and performances.

In the same vein, they also share with Geertz an affinity for cultural relativism*—the need to understand other societies through the values those societies hold. In the age of globalization—the trend toward increasingly close cultural, economic, and political ties across continental boundaries—*The Interpretation of Cultures* continues to help us understand difference, in particular "different conceptions of the self, of morality, of emotions, of religions, of political authority, of kinship, of time, as made manifest by groups of people, ways of life."[4] *The Interpretation of Cultures* remains widely debated and cited inside and outside of anthropology.

> *"Whatever the infirmities of the concept of 'culture' [...] are, there is nothing for it but to persist in spite of them."*
> —— Sherry Ortner, "Special Issue: The Fate of 'Culture': Geertz and beyond"

Interaction

Interpretive scholars across disciplines endorse Geertz's insistence on understanding meaning. They respect him as a brilliant "cultural theorist, an ethnographer, and a moral philosopher."[5]

Still, the Geertzian concept of culture has given rise to passionate debates among interpretive scholars. They argue that Geertz's classic definition of what culture is has proven less and less relevant to the modern world.[6] These scholars note that today's

145

world contains fewer distinct and recognizable cultures and fewer coherent ways of life. Scholars also find beliefs, practices, and feelings have become less unified even within a family unit, not to mention the larger groupings of tribe, community, nation, or civilization.[7] They also agree that culture appears in new fluid and complex social formations today. The characteristics of the modern "tribes" formed by global networks, social media communities, and mixed identities include globalization, complexity, and vastness.[8] Current social and political phenomena seriously call into question the usefulness of Geertz's concept of culture as unified, static, and uncontaminated by outside forces.

As a result, scholars have devoted a considerable amount of time to research rethinking and modernizing the notion of cultural systems.[9] Like Geertz, many modern ethnographers continue to study the distinct ways in which people in different localities experience their lives. Unlike Geertz, they do not view cultures as bounded and isolated. If they supplement the Geertzian approach they do so by looking at wider political, economic, social, historical, and cultural frameworks that affect local cultures and their interplay with power.[10]

The Continuing Debate

Renowned present-day cultural anthropologists such as Sherry Ortner,* Lila Abu-Lughod,* George Marcus,* or Renato Rosaldo Jr.* have discussed a variety of practical responses to the "profound and far-reaching" critiques of Geertz's concept of culture.[11] Key topics in the debate include the reconfiguration of anthropology's core concept of culture and the realities for ethnography* in the face of globalization. They have also reexamined practical forms of modern anthropological fieldwork.[12]

The influential contemporary cultural anthropologist Sherry Ortner studied with Geertz. She has produced useful summaries of the ongoing debate and reflected on a productive way forward.[13] Ortner argues that the issue should not be whether to banish or to hold on to a Geertzian concept of culture, and by extension, the classic "anthropological project."[14] She makes the extremely valid point that "the issue is, once again, one of reconfiguring this enormously productive concept for a changing world, a changing relationship between politics and academic life, and a changing landscape of theoretical possibilities."[15]

Ortner suggests three imperatives for rethinking culture.[16] First, she proposes "to maintain a strong presumption of cultural difference, but make it do new kinds of work."[17] Second, Ortner argues that modern thinkers should focus on the issue of making meaning in *The Interpretation of Cultures*, rather than the notion of cultural systems. And third, she claims that scholars should situate their cultural analysis "within and, as it were, beneath larger analyses of social and political events and processes" because "cultural analysis can no longer ... be an end in itself."[18] In other words, she calls on scholars to value the "meaning-laden" and "meaning-making" aspects of the Geertzian view. But she recognizes that they must seek to locate (in the sense of "detect" or "identify") and examine culture in new and different ways.

1. Pauline Turner Strong, "Book Review Essays: Anthropology and the Future of (Inter) Disciplinarity," *American Anthropologist* 110, no. 2 (June 2008): 253.

2. Sherry Ortner, "Special Issue: The Fate of 'Culture': Geertz and beyond," *Representations* 59 (1997), 1–14.

3. Ortner, "Special Issue," 6.

4. Richard Shweder, "The Resolute Irresolution of Clifford Geertz," *Common Knowledge* 13, nos. 2–3 (Spring-Fall 2007), 203.

5. Ortner, "Special Issue," 2.

6. Ortner, "Special Issue," 7.

7. Ortner, "Special Issue," 7.

8. Ortner, "Special Issue," 7–8.

9. Ortner, "Special Issue," 1.

10. Ortner, "Special Issue," 7–8.

11. Ortner, "Special Issue," 8.

12. Ortner, "Special Issue," 7–9.

13. Ortner, "Special Issue," 1–14.

14. Ortner, "Special Issue," 1–14.

15. Ortner, "Special Issue," 8.

16. Ortner, "Special Issue," 8.

17. Ortner, "Special Issue," 8.

18. Ortner, "Special Issue," 9.

MODULE 12
WHERE NEXT?

KEY POINTS

* *The Interpretation of Cultures* will continue to be remembered as a classic work valuing the aspects of social life associated with the production and the transmission of meaning.

* This seminal work continues to be useful in addressing "issues of social and moral philosophy." That usefulness seems unlikely to diminish.

* In *The Interpretation of Cultures* Geertz set out to establish what culture is and how it should be studied, introducing the concept of thick description—the detailed, interpretive analysis of human behavior in context.

Potential

Scholars will continue to remember Clifford Geertz's *The Interpretation of Cultures* as a classic, and Geertz himself has been credited with "reconfiguring, almost single-handedly, the boundary between the social sciences and the humanities for the second half of the twentieth century."[1] While much about the world has changed since Geertz wrote the book, this work will continue to serve as a key reference for a larger, ongoing debate about culture. Geertz's central proposition has a timeless quality and universal applicability. As his student Sherry Ortner* wrote, he wanted to understand the human condition "as defined by the constant production and transformation of meaning."[2] Geertz proposed the idea that every material, political, social, or intimate aspect of human existence is "at the same time culturally defined, shaped, and laden with cognitive and affective meaning." Scholars will likely continue to see the ripple effect of this notion across academic disciplines for the foreseeable future.[3]

Still, some scholars have pointed out deficits in the work. They note that *The Interpretation of Cultures* neglects issues of power, conflict, and inequality.[4] Critics have said it is not politically progressive, too ethically neutral, too invested in a certain concept of culture, and too descriptive where it should be explanatory.[5] Still, scholars assert that *The Interpretation of Cultures* has important implications for the politics of anthropology as a science as well as the politics within the field of anthropology. These will remain relevant in the future.[6] The work's theoretical usefulness in addressing "issues of social and moral philosophy" also remains unlikely to diminish.[7]

For that reason, Ortner proposes that when we value the "meaning-laden" and "meaning-making" aspects of social life (those parts of social life to do with the transmission or production of meaning), we continue to assume a "fundamentally Geertzian view."[8]

"Culture, if it is to continue to be understood as a vital part of the social process, must be located and examined in very different ways: as the clash of meanings in borderlands; as public culture that has its own textual coherence but is always locally interpreted; as fragile webs of story and meaning woven by vulnerable actors in nightmarish situations; as the grounds of agency and intentionality in ongoing social practice."

—— Sherry Ortner, "Special Issue: The Fate of 'Culture':
Geertz and beyond"

Future Directions

Future uses for this work will almost certainly be characterized by anthropological self-questioning. We will likely see further attempts to upgrade the Geertzian concept of culture. Scholars may also attempt to reconfigure his understanding of anthropology in relation to the multidimensional social formations that have emerged since Geertz wrote this work. These complex formations include nations, transnational networks, changing discourses (the systems of language and assumptions that we draw on when we think or talk about certain subjects), global "flows" (the movement of goods, people, ideas, technology, and so on), increasingly mixed identities, social media groups, and so forth.

Ortner sums up the overarching questions that will guide future scholars:"How can anthropology hold on to ethnographic* work in the deepest sense—long-term, intense, linguistically competent, whole-self, participant observation*—in a world of these kinds of forms and processes? What kinds of relationship(s) can/may/should obtain between the resolute localness and face-to-faceness of ethnographic work and the vastness, complexity, and especially non-localness of such formations?"[9]

Some recent cultural scholars do not see their work as engaging with the Geertzian perspective. In fact, they do not consider that they engage with cultural anthropology at all. But modern cultural anthropologists such as Sherry Ortner, Renato Rosaldo Jr.,* and Lila Abu-Lughod* point toward a direction that welcomes "the ethnographies and histories of zones of friction between cultures, in which the clash of power and meaning and identities is the stuff of change and transformation."[10] For example, Ortner wrote a book examining the history of encounters in Himalayan mountaineering.[11] On the one side, she discusses Western mountaineers. These men appear rather "savage" in her account. For one thing, they insist on slaughtering animals for meat during their expeditions. On the other side she finds Buddhist Sherpas*—inhabitants of the region around Mount Everest. These men have a profound aversion to killing, although they are not exactly nonviolent themselves.

Summary

In *The Interpretation of Cultures*, Clifford Geertz took on the intellectual challenge of identifying "what culture is, what role it plays in social life, and how it ought properly to be studied."[12] Geertz's particular approach to the study of culture centered on unraveling the webs of subjectively held meaning that groups of people share. Geertz examined the symbols of a culture and found that they embody systems of meanings.[13]

Above all, the seminal text contributed to an emerging trend of modern cultural anthropology in the twentieth-century United States. Geertz helped his peers focus how people see themselves and the world in which they live. He paid special attention to symbols such as crafts and myths. Most famously, *The Interpretation of Cultures* introduced the notion of thick description. Geertz used this interpretive process to explain the shared meaning that specific symbolic acts hold for the individuals whose actions they are. Thick description facilitates his attempts to state "what the knowledge thus attained demonstrates about the society in which it is found and, beyond that, about social life as such."[14] For many inside and outside the field, thick description came to explain not only what Geertz did but also what cultural anthropologists in general do.[15] Thick description focused on meaning-making—the way that actions come to acquire symbolic weight—and interpretation. This brought cultural anthropology closer to the humanities than the natural sciences. With his peers Marshall Sahlins,* David Schneider,* Victor Turner,* and Mary Douglas,* Geertz became known as a major voice of the 1960s "symbolic"* or "interpretive"* school of thought.

---

1. Sherry Ortner, "Special Issue: The Fate of 'Culture': Geertz and beyond," *Representations* 59 (1997): 1.

2. Sherry Ortner, "Clifford Geertz (1926–2006)," *American Anthropologist* 109, no. 4 (2007), 786.

3. Ortner, "Clifford Geertz (1926–2006)," 787.

4. Edward Bruner, "Book Review: Clifford Geertz: His Critics and Followers, 1998," *Anthropology and Humanism* 23, no. 2 (1998): 216.

5. Aram Yengoyan, "Clifford Geertz, Cultural Portraits, and Southeast Asia," *The Journal of Asian Studies* 68, no. 4 (November 2009): 1217.

6. Ortner, "Special Issue," 4.

7. Ortner, "Special Issue," 5.

8. Ortner, "Special Issue," 11.

9. Ortner, "Special Issue," 7–8.

10. Ortner, "Special Issue," 8.

11. Sherry Ortner, *Life and Death on Mt. Everest: Sherpas and Himalayan Mountaineering* (Princeton: Princeton University Press, 1999).

12. Clifford Geertz, *The Interpretation of Cultures*, 2nd edn (New York: Basic Books, 2000), vii.

13. Geertz, *The Interpretation of Cultures*, 125.

14. Geertz, *The Interpretation of Cultures*, 26–7.

15. Ortner, "Clifford Geertz (1926–2006)," 787.

◆◆— GLOSSARY OF TERMS —◆◆

1. **Anti-Semitism:** discrimination against or prejudice or hostility toward Jews.

2. **Archaeological anthropology:** the study of the origin, growth, and development of human culture from the distant past.

3. **Biological anthropology:** the study of how the human species evolved.

4. **Buddhist Sherpas:** people who inhabit the regions surrounding Mount Everest and adhere to the religious traditions of Tibetan Buddhism.

5. **Cognitive anthropology:** the branch of anthropology that examines how what people know shapes the way they perceive their surroundings and relate to the world.

6. **Cold War:** a period of tension from 1947 to 1991 between the United States and its Western allies and the Eastern federation of countries known as the Soviet Union.

7. **Colonialism:** the practice of forcibly gaining control over another country, populating it with nonnative settlers, and appropriating its resources and assets.

8. **Contextual:** based on the circumstances and context.

9. **Cultural anthropology:** the branch of anthropology that looks at the roots, history, and development of human culture.

10. **Culture:** according to Geertz, a system of shared meaning that ought to be studied by interpreting the symbols of that culture, such as art and myths.

11. **Cyberbullying:** practice common among young people in Western societies of isolating and picking on members of their peer group via online interactions using computers and mobile phones.

12. **Ecological anthropology:** a discipline studying the relationship between humans and their biophysical environment.

13. **Empyrean:** of or relating to heaven.

14. **Ethnography:** research that explores cultural phenomena and documents its findings in written field studies or case studies.

15. **Functionalism:** a viewpoint analyzing society in terms of how its elements

function.

16. **Global warming:** a rise in temperatures in the Earth's atmosphere with potentially very serious effects and caused in part by an increase in atmospheric greenhouse gases due to human activity.

17. **Historical particularism:** a belief that every society is the product of its particular historical journey.

18. **Holistic:** the belief that the parts of something are intimately interconnected and explicable only by reference to the whole.

19. *Iklas:* the Javanese concept of a detached acceptance of death.

20. **Indonesia:** an archipelago of thousands of islands in southeast Asia organized as a sovereign state, the Republic of Indonesia.

21. **Interdisciplinary:** research that draws on the aims and methods of several different academic disciplines.

22. **Interpretive approach or interpretivism:** in anthropology, an approach that believes that anthropologists should understand how peoples and cultures see themselves, and then translate the cultural meanings to outsiders.

23. **Linguistic anthropology:** the study of language as it represents culture.

24. **Marxism:** a socioeconomic and political world view developed in the nineteenth century by the German political philosopher Karl Marx, based on his propositions of how capitalism developed and shaped the struggle of the classes.

25. **Materialism:** a view that holds that nothing exists except matter, and therefore things can only be measured or known through the senses.

26. **Natural science:** a branch of science that seeks to describe, predict, and understand natural phenomena and reveal the "laws of nature."

27. **Participant observation:** a data-collection method by which researchers live among the people they study, observe them, and participate in their social life.

28. **Particularism:** the exclusive attachment to one's own interest, group, party, or nation.

29. **Positivism:** a standpoint that rejects introspective and intuitive knowledge. Positivists believe that only logical and mathematical methods are scientific and trustworthy enough in uncovering the laws of society.

30. **Postcolonialism:** an intellectual direction (sometimes also referred to as an "era" or "theory") that arose around the middle of the twentieth century when formerly colonized countries became independent. As an intellectual approach, postcolonial studies analyzes the various cultural, linguistic, and social legacies of the colonial period.

31. **Relativism:** the concept that points of view have no absolute truth or validity, but only relative, subjective value according to how different people perceive and consider them.

32. **Rendition:** a performance or interpretation, especially of a dramatic role or piece of music.

33. *Rukun:* the Javanese concept of communal harmony.

34. **Semiotics:** the study of signs and sign systems, both linguistic and nonlinguistic, in relation to the way they are transmitted.

35. **Social anthropology:** the study of social structures and their role in human cultures.

36. **Social revolution:** a revolution by the people (rather than, say, political parties) that aims to reorganize society, such as the civil rights movements in the United States in 1954–68.

37. **Sociology:** the study of social behavior, social institutions, and the origins and organization of human society.

38. **Structuralism:** the theory that we must understand elements of human culture in terms of their relationship to a larger, overarching system or structure.

39. **Subjectivity:** the notion that a person's perspective is shaped by his or her personal and unique feelings, experiences, beliefs, and desires.

40. **Symbolic anthropology:** the branch of anthropology that views culture as a set of symbolic systems, and studies rituals and symbols to unpick their cultural meanings.

41. **Thick description:** a description that explains not just a particular human behavior, but also its context, in a way that makes the behavior meaningful to an outsider.

42. *Verstehen*: German word meaning the emphatic understanding of human behavior.

43. **Virtual friends:** people known via online interactions on social networking services, message boards, shared-interest websites, and so on.

44. **World War II (1939–45):** a global conflict between the Axis Powers (Germany, Italy, and Japan) and the ultimately victorious Allied Powers (the United Kingdom and its colonies, the Soviet Union, and the United States).

PEOPLE MENTIONED IN THE TEXT

1. **Lila Abu-Lughod (b. 1952)** is an American anthropologist with Palestinian and Jewish ancestry. Her research interests focus on nationalism, media, gender politics, and the politics of memory. She wrote the much-reprinted article "Do Muslim Women Really Need Saving?" (2002).

2. **Talal Asad (b. 1932)** is an anthropologist who is known for his writings on postcolonialism, Christianity, Islam, and ritual studies.

3. **Jane Austen (1775–1817)** was an English novelist. She is the author of *Sense and Sensibility* (1811), *Pride and Prejudice* (1813), and *Emma* (1815), among other novels.

4. **Karen Blu (b. 1941)** is emerita anthropology professor at New York University. She is well known for her research on the American Indian people.

5. **Franz Boas (1858–1942)** was the founder of modern American anthropology. He established the concept of cultural relativity, and argued that all humans have the same intellectual capacity. In 1920, he wrote the programmatic essay "The Methods of Ethnology."

6. **Pierre Bourdieu (1930–2002)** was a French sociologist, philosopher, and anthropologist. Bourdieu published some 30 books and more than 300 articles on an astounding variety of topics. His empirically rich yet theoretically dense style can deter some readers.

7. **Mary Douglas (1921–2007)** was a British anthropologist. Her group/grid pattern laid the foundation for cultural theory, and her work on risk analysis pioneered economic anthropology. Her best-known book remains *Purity and Danger: An Analysis of Concepts of Pollution and Taboo*, first published in 1966.

8. **Louis Dumont (1911–98)** was a French anthropologist specializing in India. He is best known to anthropologists for his work on Indian caste and kinship.

9. **Émile Durkheim (1858–1917)** was a French sociologist, psychologist, and philosopher. Together with the political philosopher Karl Marx and the sociologist Max Weber, Durkheim is famous for founding modern sociology. He is best known for his book *Suicide* (1897), an exploration of suicides in different populations.

10. **Charles Frake (b. 1930)** was a linguistic anthropologist of the twentieth century. In 1969 he published "The Ethnographic Study of Cognitive Systems."

11. **Sigmund Freud (1856–1939)** was an Austrian neurologist, now known as the founder of modern psychoanalysis.

12. **Hildred Storey Geertz (b. 1929)** is professor emeritus of anthropology at Princeton University, where she delivers classes on the history of anthropological theory, the anthropology of art, and the art of ethnography. She has conducted fieldwork in Java, Morocco, and Bali.

13. **George R. Geiger (1903–98)** was a professor of philosophy at Antioch College. He joined the faculty in 1937 on the recommendation of the noted philosopher John Dewey and continued teaching part time even after his formal retirement in 1969. He became one of the most famous "interpreters" of the philosophy of Henry George.

14. **Marvin Harris (1927–2001)** was an American anthropologist influential in the development of cultural materialism. He wrote the defining work *The Rise of Anthropological Theory: A History of Theories of Culture*.

15. **Roger Keesing (1935–93)** was an anthropologist who is best known for his research on the Kwaio people of Malaita in the Solomon Islands. His studies are concerned with kinship, religion, politics, and language.

16. **Clyde Kluckhohn (1905–60)** was a professor in social anthropology and social relations at Harvard University. He is best known for studying the language and culture of the Navajo, and for developing a methodological approach called the Values Orientation Theory.

17. **Claude Lévi-Strauss (1908–2009)** was a French social anthropologist and is associated with founding and advocating structuralism, which analyzes the structures of cultural systems such as kinship.

18. **George Marcus (b. 1968)** is an American cultural anthropologist with a research interest in power and its effects on ordinary people. Marcus also founded the journal *Cultural Anthropology* in 1986.

19. **Bronisław Malinowski (1884–1942)** was one of the most influential

anthropologists of the twentieth century. He is known for founding social anthropology and conducted most of his research on the peoples of Oceania.

20. **Karl Marx (1818–83)** was a philosopher, sociologist, and economist. Most people know him for being a revolutionary communist because his writings were the foundation for many communist regimes in the twentieth century. His main work is *Das Kapital* ("Capital"), published in three volumes in 1867–94.

21. **C. Wright Mills (1916–62)** was an American sociologist, who worked at Columbia University from 1946 until his death. His best-known publications include *White Collar* (1951), *The Power Elite* (1956), and *The Sociological Imagination* (1959).

22. **Sherry Ortner (b. 1941)** is a cultural anthropologist who studied with Geertz and is best known for her theories on transformation and resistance.

23. **Talcott Parsons (1902–79)** is widely considered one of the twentieth century's most influential American sociologists. He was responsible for introducing the pioneering sociologist Max Weber to American scholarship, and also argued for a focus on people's subjective realities. His major works included *The Structure of Social Action* (1937) and *The Social System* (1951).

24. **Alfred Radcliffe-Brown (1881–1955)** was an English social anthropologist. His work was concerned with how the social structures of preindustrial societies functioned. On this basis, he developed his theory of functionalism.

25. **Roy Rappaport (1926–97)** was an anthropologist who particularly contributed to the study of rituals and ecological anthropology.

26. **Richard Rorty (1931–2007)** was an influential, pragmatic American philosopher. His major works included *Philosophy and the Mirror of Nature* (1979).

27. **Renato Rosaldo Jr. (b. 1941)** is one of the world's leading cultural anthropologists, with a particular interest in cultural citizenship.

28. **Gilbert Ryle (1900–76)** was an English philosopher concerned with the nature and use of language. Principally known for asserting that the workings of the mind remain connected to the actions of the body, he is best known for his book *The Concept of Mind* (1949).

29. **Marshall Sahlins (b. 1930)** is an anthropologist at the University of Chicago. His work focuses on the power of culture in shaping people's perceptions and actions.

30. **Ferdinand de Saussure (1857–1913)** was a Swiss linguist who is considered a founding father of modern linguistics and the study of meaning-making or signification. He is best known for his posthumously published lectures on linguistics.

31. **David M. Schneider (1918–95)** was a major proponent of the symbolic anthropological approach, and is particularly known for his studies on kinship.

32. **Richard Shweder (b. 1945)** is an American cultural anthropologist who wrote *Thinking through Cultures: Expeditions in Cultural Psychology* (1991) and *Why Do Men Barbecue? Recipes for Cultural Psychology* (2003).

33. **James Spradley (1933–82)** was a prolific American anthropologist who believed that researchers should look for the meaning that participants make of their lives.

34. **Victor Turner (1920–83)** was a Scottish anthropologist who is famous for his research on rituals and rites of passage.

35. **Edward Burnett Tylor (1832–1917)** was an English anthropologist who is credited with founding cultural anthropology. His most influential work remains *Primitive Culture* (1871).

36. **Andrew P. Vayda (b. 1931)** is an ecological anthropologist, specializing in methodology and explanation. He primarily explores the interface between social and ecological science in Indonesia and Papua New Guinea.

37. **Max Weber (1864–1920)** was a German sociologist. Scholars consider him one of the three founding architects of sociology, along with the French social theorist Émile Durkheim and the German political philosopher Karl Marx. He is known for his ideas on bureaucracy and his most influential essay "The Protestant Ethic and the Spirit of Capitalism" (1934).

38. **Aram Yengoyan (b. 1936)** is an American professor in anthropology with particular expertise in Southeast Asia.

WORKS CITED

1. Alexander, Jeffrey, Philip Smith, Matthew Norton, and Peter Brooks, eds. *Interpreting Clifford Geertz: Cultural Investigation in the Social Sciences.* New York: Palgrave Macmillan, 2011.

2. Asad, Talal. "Anthropological Conceptions of Religion: Reflections on Geertz." *Man* 18, no. 2 (1983): 237–59.

3. Bourdieu, Pierre. *Distinction: A Social Critique of the Judgement of Taste.* Translated by Richard Nice. Cambridge, MA: Harvard University Press, 1987.

4. Bruner, Edward. "Book Review: Clifford Geertz: His Critics and Followers, 1998." *Anthropology and Humanism* 23, no. 2 (1998): 215–16.

5. Geertz, Clifford. *After the Fact: Two Countries, Four Decades, One Anthropologist.* Cambridge, MA: Harvard University Press, 1995.

6. ____. *Agricultural Involution: The Processes of Ecological Change in Indonesia.* Los Angeles: University of California Press, 1963.

7. ____. *Available Light: Anthropological Reflections on Philosophical Topics.* Princeton: Princeton University Press, 2000.

8. ____. *The Interpretation of Cultures.* 2nd edn. New York: Basic Books, 2000.

9. ____. *Islam Observed: Religious Development in Morocco and Indonesia.* New Haven: Yale University Press, 1968.

10. ____. *Kinship in Bali.* Chicago: University of Chicago Press, 1975.

11. ____. *Life among the Anthros and Other Essays.* Princeton: Princeton University Press, 2010.

12. ____. *Local Knowledge: Further Essays in Interpretive Anthropology.* New York: Basic Books, 1983.

13. ____. "Passage and Accident: A Life of Learning." In *Available Light: Anthropological Reflections on Philosophical Topics*, by Clifford Geertz. Princeton: Princeton University Press, 2000.

14. ____. *Peddlers and Princes: Social Development and Economic Change in Two Indonesian Towns.* Chicago: University of Chicago Press, 1963.

15. ____. *Person, Time, and Conduct in Bali: An Essay in Cultural Analysis*. New Haven: Yale University Southeast Asia Studies, 1966.

16. ____. *The Religion of Java*. Glencoe: The Free Press, 1960.

17. ____. *Works and Lives: The Anthropologist as Author*. Stanford: Stanford University Press, 1988.

18. Geertz, Clifford, ed. *Myth, Symbol, and Culture*. New York: Norton, 1971.

19. Geertz, Clifford, Hildred Geertz, and Lawrence Rosen. *Meaning and Order in Moroccan Society*. New York: Cambridge University Press, 1979.

20. Institute for Advanced Study. "Clifford Geertz 1926–2006." Accessed December 8, 2015. https://www.ias.edu/news/press-releases/2009–49.

21. Keesing, Roger. "Theories of Culture." *Annual Review of Anthropology* 3 (1974): 73–97.

22. Kronenfeld, David, Giovanni Bennardo, Victor de Munck, and Michael Fischer, eds. *A Companion to Cognitive Anthropology*. Singapore: Blackwell Publishing Ltd., 2011.

23. Leopold, Joan. *Culture in Comparative and Evolutionary Perspective: E. B. Tylor and the Making of Primitive Culture*. Berlin: Dietrich Reimer Verlag, 1980.

24. Lévi-Strauss, Claude. *The Savage Mind*. Chicago: University of Chicago Press, 1966.

25. Lewis, Diane. "Anthropology and Colonialism." *Current Anthropology* 14, no. 5 (December 1973): 581–602.

26. Mills, C. Wright. *The Sociological Imagination*. New York: Oxford University Press, 1959.

27. Ortner, Sherry. "Clifford Geertz (1926–2006)." *American Anthropologist* 109, no. 4 (2007): 786–98.

28. ____. *Life and Death on Mt. Everest: Sherpas and Himalayan Mountaineering*. Princeton: Princeton University Press, 1999.

29. ____. "Special Issue: The Fate of 'Culture': Geertz and beyond." *Representations* 59 (1997): 1–14.

30. Parsons, Talcott. *The Social System.* New York: Free Press, 1951.

31. Rosaldo, Renato Jr. "Geertz's Gifts." *Common Knowledge* 13, nos. 2–3 (2007).

32. Ryle, Gilbert. *The Concept of Mind.* Chicago: University of Chicago Press, 1949.

33. Sahlins, Marshall. *Culture and Practical Reason.* Chicago: University of Chicago Press, 1978.

34. Schneider, David. *American Kinship: A Cultural Account.* 2nd edn. Chicago: University of Chicago Press, 1980.

35. Shweder, Richard. "Clifford Geertz." *Proceedings of the American Philosophical Society* 154, no. 1 (March 2010): 87–93.

36. ____. *Clifford James Geertz: 1926–2006, A Biographical Memoir.* Washington, DC: National Academy of Sciences. Accessed November 2, 2015. https://www.sss.ias.edu/files/pdfs/Geertz_NAS_6–10–10.pdf.

37. ____. "The Resolute Irresolution of Clifford Geertz." *Common Knowledge* 13, nos. 2–3 (Spring-Fall 2007): 191–205.

38. Shweder, Richard, and Byron Good, eds. *Clifford Geertz by His Colleagues.* Chicago: University of Chicago Press, 2005.

39. Turner Strong, Pauline. "Book Review Essays: Anthropology and the Future of (Inter) Disciplinarity." *American Anthropologist* 110, no. 2 (June 2008): 253.

40. Tylor, Edward Burnett. *Primitive Culture: Researches into the Development of Mythology, Philosophy, Religion, Language, Art and Custom.* 2 vols. London: John Murray 1871.

41. Weber, Max. *The Protestant Ethic and the Spirit of Capitalism.* Translated by Talcott Parsons. London, New York: Routledge, 2001.

42. Yarrow, Andrew. "Clifford Geertz, Cultural Anthropologist, Is Dead at 80." *New York Times*, November 1, 2006. Accessed December 8, 2015. http://www.nytimes.com/2006/11/01/obituaries/01geertz.html?pagewanted=print&_r=0

43. Yengoyan, Aram. "Clifford Geertz, Cultural Portraits, and Southeast Asia." *The Journal of Asian Studies* 68, no. 4 (November 2009): 1215–30.

原书作者简介

人类学家克利福德·格尔茨1926年出生于美国旧金山。父母离异后，他在加州农村的一个寄养家庭长大，并在二战期间服了两年兵役。随后，他获得了哈佛大学人类学博士学位。

哈佛大学当时新成立的社会关系学院采用跨学科的方法来研究人类学。在格尔茨漫长的学术生涯中，这一在当时标新立异的观念奠定了他的工作与成就。在他的职业生涯中，他曾在普林斯顿大学高等研究学院担任了30年的社会科学教授。除此之外，格尔茨也是一位著作甚丰的实地调研员和作家——正如他的一位同事所言，他是"20世纪一位重要的知识分子"。格尔茨于2006年辞世。

本书作者简介

阿贝娜·达兹-阿瑟博士拥有伦敦政治经济学院当代政治社会学硕士学位和伯明翰大学文化公共管理博士学位。目前，她是伯明翰大学政府与社会学院的一名讲师。

世界名著中的批判性思维

《世界思想宝库钥匙丛书》致力于深入浅出地阐释全世界著名思想家的观点，不论是谁、在何处都能了解到，从而推进批判性思维发展。

《世界思想宝库钥匙丛书》与世界顶尖大学的一流学者合作，为一系列学科中最有影响的著作推出新的分析文本，介绍其观点和影响。在这一不断扩展的系列中，每种选入的著作都代表了历经时间考验的思想典范。通过为这些著作提供必要背景、揭示原作者的学术渊源以及说明这些著作所产生的影响，本系列图书希望让读者以新视角看待这些划时代的经典之作。读者应学会思考、运用并挑战这些著作中的观点，而不是简单接受它们。

ABOUT THE AUTHOR OF THE ORIGINAL WORK

Born in San Francisco in 1926, American anthropologist **Clifford Geertz** was raised in a foster family in rural California after his parents divorced. Completing two years of military service during World War II, he went on to earn a PhD in anthropology from Harvard.

Harvard's newly formed Department of Social Relations took an interdisciplinary approach to anthropology, and this idea, which was novel at the time, shaped Geertz's work throughout his long academic career. That career included 30 years as professor of social science at Princeton University's Institute for Advanced Study, but Geertz was also a prolific field researcher and author. A 'major intellectual figure of the twentieth century' — as one colleague called him — Geertz died in 2006.

ABOUT THE AUTHOR OF THE ANALYSIS

Dr Abena Dadze-Arthur holds an MSc in contemporary political sociology from the London School of Economics and a doctorate in culturally-rooted public management from the University of Birmingham. She is currently a lecturer in the School of Government and Society at Birmingham.

ABOUT MACAT
GREAT WORKS FOR CRITICAL THINKING

Macat is focused on making the ideas of the world's great thinkers accessible and comprehensible to everybody, everywhere, in ways that promote the development of enhanced critical thinking skills.

It works with leading academics from the world's top universities to produce new analyses that focus on the ideas and the impact of the most influential works ever written across a wide variety of academic disciplines. Each of the works that sit at the heart of its growing library is an enduring example of great thinking. But by setting them in context — and looking at the influences that shaped their authors, as well as the responses they provoked — Macat encourages readers to look at these classics and game-changers with fresh eyes. Readers learn to think, engage and challenge their ideas, rather than simply accepting them.

批判性思维与《文化的解释》

首要批判性思维技巧：阐释

次要批判性思维技巧：创造性思维

克利福德·格尔茨被誉为"他这一代人中最具原创性的人类学家"——这一美誉在很大程度上源于他在《文化的解释》一书中阐述的人类学解释性方法的巨大贡献。

解释性方法在人类学中的地位举足轻重，这一点无可争议：在一门关于理解人类并试图勾勒各文化间的差异性和共性的学科中，解释是至关重要的技能。然而，对于格尔茨而言，标准的解释性方法还不够深入，他毕生的工作都集中在不断深化和完善有关解释能力的研究课题上。

格尔茨最著名的贡献是他对"文化"的定义，以及他的"深描"理论——一种基于解释性方法并产生了影响的新型技能。对于格尔茨而言，"文化"就好比一张"意义之网"，每个人都身处其中。因此，理解文化与其说是探索规律，不如说是建立一个解释性的框架，这一框架直接关注对给定文化中事物的真正意义加以界定。在格尔茨看来，实现这一目标的最佳途径就是"深描"，一种通过探索语境和环境，在文化的意义之网中阐明意义的记录事物的方式。这是格尔茨的重大创新，意义深远且具有开拓性，值得所有批判性思想家学习。

CRITICAL THINKING AND *THE INTERPRETATION OF CULTURES*

- Primary critical thinking skill: INTERPRETATION
- Secondary critical thinking skill: CREATIVE THINKING

Clifford Geertz has been called "the most original anthropologist of his generation" — and this reputation rests largely on the huge contributions to the methodology and approaches of anthropological interpretation that he outlined in *The Interpretation of Cultures*.

The centrality of interpretative skills to anthropology is uncontested: in a subject that is all about understanding mankind, and which seeks to outline the differences and the common ground that exists between cultures, interpretation is the crucial skillset. For Geertz, however, standard interpretative approaches did not go deep enough, and his life's work concentrated on deepening and perfecting his subject's interpretative skills.

Geertz is best known for his definition of "culture," and his theory of "thick description," an influential technique that depends on fresh interpretative approaches. For Geertz, "cultures" are "webs of meaning" in which everyone is suspended. Understanding culture, therefore, is not so much a matter of going in search of law, but of setting out an interpretative framework for meaning that focuses directly on attempts to define the real meaning of things within a given culture. The best way to do this, for Geertz, is via "thick description": a way of recording things that explores context and surroundings, and articulates meaning within the web of culture. Ambitious and bold, Geertz's greatest creation is a method all critical thinkers can learn from.

《世界思想宝库钥匙丛书》简介

《世界思想宝库钥匙丛书》致力于为一系列在各领域产生重大影响的人文社科类经典著作提供独特的学术探讨。每一本读物都不仅仅是原经典著作的内容摘要，而是介绍并深入研究原经典著作的学术渊源、主要观点和历史影响。这一丛书的目的是提供一套学习资料，以促进读者掌握批判性思维，从而更全面、深刻地去理解重要思想。

每一本读物分为 3 个部分：学术渊源、学术思想和学术影响，每个部分下有 4 个小节。这些章节旨在从各个方面研究原经典著作及其反响。

由于独特的体例，每一本读物不但易于阅读，而且另有一项优点：所有读物的编排体例相同，读者在进行某个知识层面的调查或研究时可交叉参阅多本该丛书中的相关读物，从而开启跨领域研究的路径。

为了方便阅读，每本读物最后还列出了术语表和人名表（在书中则以星号 * 标记），此外还有参考文献。

《世界思想宝库钥匙丛书》与剑桥大学合作，理清了批判性思维的要点，即如何通过 6 种技能来进行有效思考。其中 3 种技能让我们能够理解问题，另 3 种技能让我们有能力解决问题。这 6 种技能合称为"批判性思维 PACIER 模式"，它们是：

分析：了解如何建立一个观点；
评估：研究一个观点的优点和缺点；
阐释：对意义所产生的问题加以理解；
创造性思维：提出新的见解，发现新的联系；
解决问题：提出切实有效的解决办法；
理性化思维：创建有说服力的观点。

THE MACAT LIBRARY

The Macat Library is a series of unique academic explorations of seminal works in the humanities and social sciences — books and papers that have had a significant and widely recognised impact on their disciplines. It has been created to serve as much more than just a summary of what lies between the covers of a great book. It illuminates and explores the influences on, ideas of, and impact of that book. Our goal is to offer a learning resource that encourages critical thinking and fosters a better, deeper understanding of important ideas.

Each publication is divided into three Sections: Influences, Ideas, and Impact. Each Section has four Modules. These explore every important facet of the work, and the responses to it.

This Section-Module structure makes a Macat Library book easy to use, but it has another important feature. Because each Macat book is written to the same format, it is possible (and encouraged!) to cross-reference multiple Macat books along the same lines of inquiry or research. This allows the reader to open up interesting interdisciplinary pathways.

To further aid your reading, lists of glossary terms and people mentioned are included at the end of this book (these are indicated by an asterisk [*] throughout) — as well as a list of works cited.

Macat has worked with the University of Cambridge to identify the elements of critical thinking and understand the ways in which six different skills combine to enable effective thinking.

Three allow us to fully understand a problem; three more give us the tools to solve it. Together, these six skills make up the PACIER model of critical thinking. They are:

ANALYSIS — understanding how an argument is built
EVALUATION — exploring the strengths and weaknesses of an argument
INTERPRETATION — understanding issues of meaning
CREATIVE THINKING — coming up with new ideas and fresh connections
PROBLEM-SOLVING — producing strong solutions
REASONING — creating strong arguments

"《世界思想宝库钥匙丛书》提供了独一无二的跨学科学习和研究工具。它介绍那些革新了各自学科研究的经典著作，还邀请全世界一流专家和教育机构进行严谨的分析，为每位读者打开世界顶级教育的大门。"

—— 安德烈亚斯·施莱歇尔，
经济合作与发展组织教育与技能司司长

"《世界思想宝库钥匙丛书》直面大学教育的巨大挑战……他们组建了一支精干而活跃的学者队伍，来推出在研究广度上颇具新意的教学材料。"

—— 布罗尔斯教授、勋爵，剑桥大学前校长

"《世界思想宝库钥匙丛书》的愿景令人赞叹。它通过分析和阐释那些曾深刻影响人类思想以及社会、经济发展的经典文本，提供了新的学习方法。它推动批判性思维，这对于任何社会和经济体来说都是至关重要的。这就是未来的学习方法。"

—— 查尔斯·克拉克阁下，英国前教育大臣

"对于那些影响了各自领域的著作，《世界思想宝库钥匙丛书》能让人们立即了解到围绕那些著作展开的评论性言论，这让该系列图书成为在这些领域从事研究的师生们不可或缺的资源。"

—— 威廉·特朗佐教授，加利福尼亚大学圣地亚哥分校

"Macat offers an amazing first-of-its-kind tool for interdisciplinary learning and research. Its focus on works that transformed their disciplines and its rigorous approach, drawing on the world's leading experts and educational institutions, opens up a world-class education to anyone."

—— Andreas Schleicher, Director for Education and Skills, Organisation for Economic Co-operation and Development

"Macat is taking on some of the major challenges in university education... They have drawn together a strong team of active academics who are producing teaching materials that are novel in the breadth of their approach."

—— Prof Lord Broers, former Vice-Chancellor of the University of Cambridge

"The Macat vision is exceptionally exciting. It focuses upon new modes of learning which analyse and explain seminal texts which have profoundly influenced world thinking and so social and economic development. It promotes the kind of critical thinking which is essential for any society and economy. This is the learning of the future."

—— Rt Hon Charles Clarke, former UK Secretary of State for Education

"The Macat analyses provide immediate access to the critical conversation surrounding the books that have shaped their respective discipline, which will make them an invaluable resource to all of those, students and teachers, working in the field."

—— Prof William Tronzo, University of California at San Diego

TITLE	中文书名	类别
An Analysis of Arjun Appadurai's *Modernity at Large: Cultural Dimensions of Globalization*	解析阿尔君·阿帕杜莱《消失的现代性：全球化的文化维度》	人类学
An Analysis of Claude Lévi-Strauss's *Structural Anthropology*	解析克劳德·列维−斯特劳斯《结构人类学》	人类学
An Analysis of Marcel Mauss's *The Gift*	解析马塞尔·莫斯《礼物》	人类学
An Analysis of Jared M. Diamond's *Guns, Germs, and Steel: The Fate of Human Societies*	解析贾雷德·M.戴蒙德《枪炮、病菌与钢铁：人类社会的命运》	人类学
An Analysis of Clifford Geertz's *The Interpretation of Cultures*	解析克利福德·格尔茨《文化的解释》	人类学
An Analysis of Philippe Ariès's *Centuries of Childhood: A Social History of Family Life*	解析菲力浦·阿利埃斯《儿童的世纪：旧制度下的儿童和家庭生活》	人类学
An Analysis of W. Chan Kim & Renée Mauborgne's *Blue Ocean Strategy*	解析全伟灿/勒妮·莫博涅《蓝海战略》	商业
An Analysis of John P. Kotter's *Leading Change*	解析约翰·P.科特《领导变革》	商业
An Analysis of Michael E. Porter's *Competitive Strategy: Techniques for Analyzing Industries and Competitors*	解析迈克尔·E.波特《竞争战略：分析产业和竞争对手的技术》	商业
An Analysis of Jean Lave & Etienne Wenger's *Situated Learning: Legitimate Peripheral Participation*	解析琼·莱夫/艾蒂纳·温格《情境学习：合法的边缘性参与》	商业
An Analysis of Douglas McGregor's *The Human Side of Enterprise*	解析道格拉斯·麦格雷戈《企业的人性面》	商业
An Analysis of Milton Friedman's *Capitalism and Freedom*	解析米尔顿·弗里德曼《资本主义与自由》	商业
An Analysis of Ludwig von Mises's *The Theory of Money and Credit*	解析路德维希·冯·米塞斯《货币和信用理论》	经济学
An Analysis of Adam Smith's *The Wealth of Nations*	解析亚当·斯密《国富论》	经济学
An Analysis of Thomas Piketty's *Capital in the Twenty-First Century*	解析托马斯·皮凯蒂《21世纪资本论》	经济学
An Analysis of Nassim Nicholas Taleb's *The Black Swan: The Impact of the Highly Improbable*	解析纳西姆·尼古拉斯·塔勒布《黑天鹅：如何应对不可预知的未来》	经济学
An Analysis of Ha-Joon Chang's *Kicking Away the Ladder*	解析张夏准《富国陷阱：发达国家为何踢开梯子》	经济学
An Analysis of Thomas Robert Malthus's *An Essay on the Principle of Population*	解析托马斯·罗伯特·马尔萨斯《人口论》	经济学

An Analysis of John Maynard Keynes's *The General Theory of Employment, Interest and Money*	解析约翰·梅纳德·凯恩斯《就业、利息和货币通论》	经济学
An Analysis of Milton Friedman's *The Role of Monetary Policy*	解析米尔顿·弗里德曼《货币政策的作用》	经济学
An Analysis of Burton G. Malkiel's *A Random Walk Down Wall Street*	解析伯顿·G.马尔基尔《漫步华尔街》	经济学
An Analysis of Friedrich A. Hayek's *The Road to Serfdom*	解析弗里德里希·A.哈耶克《通往奴役之路》	经济学
An Analysis of Charles P. Kindleberger's *Manias, Panics, and Crashes: A History of Financial Crises*	解析查尔斯·P.金德尔伯格《疯狂、惊恐和崩溃：金融危机史》	经济学
An Analysis of Amartya Sen's *Development as Freedom*	解析阿马蒂亚·森《以自由看待发展》	经济学
An Analysis of Rachel Carson's *Silent Spring*	解析蕾切尔·卡森《寂静的春天》	地理学
An Analysis of Charles Darwin's *On the Origin of Species: by Means of Natural Selection, or The Preservation of Favoured Races in the Struggle for Life*	解析查尔斯·达尔文《物种起源》	地理学
An Analysis of World Commission on Environment and Development's *The Brundtland Report: Our Common Future*	解析世界环境与发展委员会《布伦特兰报告：我们共同的未来》	地理学
An Analysis of James E. Lovelock's *Gaia: A New Look at Life on Earth*	解析詹姆斯·E.拉伍洛克《盖娅：地球生命的新视野》	地理学
An Analysis of Paul Kennedy's *The Rise and Fall of the Great Powers: Economic Change and Military Conflict from 1500–2000*	解析保罗·肯尼迪《大国的兴衰：1500—2000年的经济变革与军事冲突》	历史
An Analysis of Janet L. Abu-Lughod's *Before European Hegemony: The World System A. D. 1250–1350*	解析珍妮特·L.阿布－卢格霍德《欧洲霸权之前：1250—1350年的世界体系》	历史
An Analysis of Alfred W. Crosby's *The Columbian Exchange: Biological and Cultural Consequences of 1492*	解析艾尔弗雷德·W.克罗斯比《哥伦布大交换：1492年以后的生物影响和文化冲击》	历史
An Analysis of Tony Judt's *Postwar: A History of Europe since 1945*	解析托尼·朱特《战后欧洲史》	历史
An Analysis of Richard J. Evans's *In Defence of History*	解析理查德·J.艾文斯《捍卫历史》	历史
An Analysis of Eric Hobsbawm's *The Age of Revolution: Europe 1789–1848*	解析艾瑞克·霍布斯鲍姆《革命的年代：欧洲 1789—1848 年》	历史

An Analysis of Roland Barthes's *Mythologies*	解析罗兰·巴特《神话学》	文学与批判理论
An Analysis of Simone de Beauvoir's *The Second Sex*	解析西蒙娜·德·波伏娃《第二性》	文学与批判理论
An Analysis of Edward W. Said's *Orientalism*	解析爱德华·W.萨义德《东方主义》	文学与批判理论
An Analysis of Virginia Woolf's *A Room of One's Own*	解析弗吉尼亚·伍尔芙《一间自己的房间》	文学与批判理论
An Analysis of Judith Butler's *Gender Trouble*	解析朱迪斯·巴特勒《性别麻烦》	文学与批判理论
An Analysis of Ferdinand de Saussure's *Course in General Linguistics*	解析费尔迪南·德·索绪尔《普通语言学教程》	文学与批判理论
An Analysis of Susan Sontag's *On Photography*	解析苏珊·桑塔格《论摄影》	文学与批判理论
An Analysis of Walter Benjamin's *The Work of Art in the Age of Mechanical Reproduction*	解析瓦尔特·本雅明《机械复制时代的艺术作品》	文学与批判理论
An Analysis of W. E. B. Du Bois's *The Souls of Black Folk*	解析W.E.B.杜波依斯《黑人的灵魂》	文学与批判理论
An Analysis of Plato's *The Republic*	解析柏拉图《理想国》	哲学
An Analysis of Plato's *Symposium*	解析柏拉图《会饮篇》	哲学
An Analysis of Aristotle's *Metaphysics*	解析亚里士多德《形而上学》	哲学
An Analysis of Aristotle's *Nicomachean Ethics*	解析亚里士多德《尼各马可伦理学》	哲学
An Analysis of Immanuel Kant's *Critique of Pure Reason*	解析伊曼努尔·康德《纯粹理性批判》	哲学
An Analysis of Ludwig Wittgenstein's *Philosophical Investigations*	解析路德维希·维特根斯坦《哲学研究》	哲学
An Analysis of G. W. F. Hegel's *Phenomenology of Spirit*	解析G.W.F.黑格尔《精神现象学》	哲学
An Analysis of Baruch Spinoza's *Ethics*	解析巴鲁赫·斯宾诺莎《伦理学》	哲学
An Analysis of Hannah Arendt's *The Human Condition*	解析汉娜·阿伦特《人的境况》	哲学
An Analysis of G. E. M. Anscombe's *Modern Moral Philosophy*	解析G.E.M.安斯康姆《现代道德哲学》	哲学
An Analysis of David Hume's *An Enquiry Concerning Human Understanding*	解析大卫·休谟《人类理解研究》	哲学

An Analysis of Søren Kierkegaard's *Fear and Trembling*	解析索伦·克尔凯郭尔《恐惧与战栗》	哲学
An Analysis of René Descartes's *Meditations on First Philosophy*	解析勒内·笛卡尔《第一哲学沉思录》	哲学
An Analysis of Friedrich Nietzsche's *On the Genealogy of Morality*	解析弗里德里希·尼采《论道德的谱系》	哲学
An Analysis of Gilbert Ryle's *The Concept of Mind*	解析吉尔伯特·赖尔《心的概念》	哲学
An Analysis of Thomas Kuhn's *The Structure of Scientific Revolutions*	解析托马斯·库恩《科学革命的结构》	哲学
An Analysis of John Stuart Mill's *Utilitarianism*	解析约翰·斯图亚特·穆勒《功利主义》	哲学
An Analysis of Aristotle's *Politics*	解析亚里士多德《政治学》	政治学
An Analysis of Niccolò Machiavelli's *The Prince*	解析尼科洛·马基雅维利《君主论》	政治学
An Analysis of Karl Marx's *Capital*	解析卡尔·马克思《资本论》	政治学
An Analysis of Benedict Anderson's *Imagined Communities*	解析本尼迪克特·安德森《想象的共同体》	政治学
An Analysis of Samuel P. Huntington's *The Clash of Civilizations and the Remaking of World Order*	解析塞缪尔·P.亨廷顿《文明的冲突与世界秩序的重建》	政治学
An Analysis of Alexis de Tocqueville's *Democracy in America*	解析阿列克西·德·托克维尔《论美国的民主》	政治学
An Analysis of John A. Hobson's *Imperialism: A Study*	解析约翰·A.霍布森《帝国主义》	政治学
An Analysis of Thomas Paine's *Common Sense*	解析托马斯·潘恩《常识》	政治学
An Analysis of John Rawls's *A Theory of Justice*	解析约翰·罗尔斯《正义论》	政治学
An Analysis of Francis Fukuyama's *The End of History and the Last Man*	解析弗朗西斯·福山《历史的终结与最后的人》	政治学
An Analysis of John Locke's *Two Treatises of Government*	解析约翰·洛克《政府论》	政治学
An Analysis of Sun Tzu's *The Art of War*	解析孙武《孙子兵法》	政治学
An Analysis of Henry Kissinger's *World Order: Reflections on the Character of Nations and the Course of History*	解析亨利·基辛格《世界秩序》	政治学
An Analysis of Jean-Jacques Rousseau's *The Social Contract*	解析让-雅克·卢梭《社会契约论》	政治学

An Analysis of Odd Arne Westad's *The Global Cold War: Third World Interventions and the Making of Our Times*	解析文安立《全球冷战：美苏对第三世界的干涉与当代世界的形成》	政治学
An Analysis of Sigmund Freud's *The Interpretation of Dreams*	解析西格蒙德·弗洛伊德《梦的解析》	心理学
An Analysis of William James' *The Principles of Psychology*	解析威廉·詹姆斯《心理学原理》	心理学
An Analysis of Philip Zimbardo's *The Lucifer Effect*	解析菲利普·津巴多《路西法效应》	心理学
An Analysis of Leon Festinger's *A Theory of Cognitive Dissonance*	解析利昂·费斯汀格《认知失调论》	心理学
An Analysis of Richard H. Thaler & Cass R. Sunstein's *Nudge: Improving Decisions about Health, Wealth, and Happiness*	解析理查德·H. 泰勒 / 卡斯·R. 桑斯坦《助推：如何做出有关健康、财富和幸福的更优决策》	心理学
An Analysis of Gordon Allport's *The Nature of Prejudice*	解析高尔登·奥尔波特《偏见的本质》	心理学
An Analysis of Steven Pinker's *The Better Angels of Our Nature: Why Violence Has Declined*	解析斯蒂芬·平克《人性中的善良天使：暴力为什么会减少》	心理学
An Analysis of Stanley Milgram's *Obedience to Authority*	解析斯坦利·米尔格拉姆《对权威的服从》	心理学
An Analysis of Betty Friedan's *The Feminine Mystique*	解析贝蒂·弗里丹《女性的奥秘》	心理学
An Analysis of David Riesman's *The Lonely Crowd: A Study of the Changing American Character*	解析大卫·理斯曼《孤独的人群：美国人社会性格演变之研究》	社会学
An Analysis of Franz Boas's *Race, Language and Culture*	解析弗朗兹·博厄斯《种族、语言与文化》	社会学
An Analysis of Pierre Bourdieu's *Outline of a Theory of Practice*	解析皮埃尔·布尔迪厄《实践理论大纲》	社会学
An Analysis of Max Weber's *The Protestant Ethic and the Spirit of Capitalism*	解析马克斯·韦伯《新教伦理与资本主义精神》	社会学
An Analysis of Jane Jacobs's *The Death and Life of Great American Cities*	解析简·雅各布斯《美国大城市的死与生》	社会学
An Analysis of C. Wright Mills's *The Sociological Imagination*	解析 C. 赖特·米尔斯《社会学的想象力》	社会学
An Analysis of Robert E. Lucas Jr.'s *Why Doesn't Capital Flow from Rich to Poor Countries?*	解析小罗伯特·E. 卢卡斯《为何资本不从富国流向穷国？》	社会学

An Analysis of Émile Durkheim's *On Suicide*	解析埃米尔·迪尔凯姆《自杀论》	社会学
An Analysis of Eric Hoffer's *The True Believer: Thoughts on the Nature of Mass Movements*	解析埃里克·霍弗《狂热分子：群众运动圣经》	社会学
An Analysis of Jared M. Diamond's *Collapse: How Societies Choose to Fail or Survive*	解析贾雷德·M.戴蒙德《大崩溃：社会如何选择兴亡》	社会学
An Analysis of Michel Foucault's *The History of Sexuality Vol. 1: The Will to Knowledge*	解析米歇尔·福柯《性史（第一卷）：求知意志》	社会学
An Analysis of Michel Foucault's *Discipline and Punish*	解析米歇尔·福柯《规训与惩罚》	社会学
An Analysis of Richard Dawkins's *The Selfish Gene*	解析理查德·道金斯《自私的基因》	社会学
An Analysis of Antonio Gramsci's *Prison Notebooks*	解析安东尼奥·葛兰西《狱中札记》	社会学
An Analysis of Augustine's *Confessions*	解析奥古斯丁《忏悔录》	神学
An Analysis of C. S. Lewis's *The Abolition of Man*	解析 C. S. 路易斯《人之废》	神学

图书在版编目（CIP）数据

解析克利福德·格尔茨《文化的解释》: 汉、英/阿贝娜·达兹-阿瑟（Abena Dadze-Arthur）著；陈运香译. —上海：上海外语教育出版社，2020
（世界思想宝库钥匙丛书）
ISBN 978-7-5446-6156-0

Ⅰ.①解… Ⅱ.①阿… ②陈… Ⅲ.①文化人类学-研究-汉、英 Ⅳ.①C958

中国版本图书馆CIP数据核字（2020）第023029号

This Chinese-English bilingual edition of *An Analysis of Clifford Geertz's* The Interpretation of Cultures is published by arrangement with Macat International Limited.
Licensed for sale throughout the world.

本书汉英双语版由Macat国际有限公司授权上海外语教育出版社有限公司出版。供在全世界范围内发行、销售。

图字：09 – 2018 – 549

出版发行：上海外语教育出版社
　　　　　　（上海外国语大学内）　邮编：200083
电　　话： 021-65425300（总机）
电子邮箱： bookinfo@sflep.com.cn
网　　址： http://www.sflep.com
责任编辑： 梁瀚杰

印　　刷： 上海叶大印务发展有限公司
开　　本： 890×1240　1/32　印张 5.875　字数 121千字
版　　次： 2020 年 9 月第 1 版　2020 年 9 月第 1 次印刷
印　　数： 2 100 册

书　　号： ISBN 978-7-5446-6156-0
定　　价： 30.00 元
　　　　本版图书如有印装质量问题，可向本社调换
　　　　质量服务热线：4008-213-263　电子邮箱：editorial@sflep.com